THE INCOMPLETE
BOOK OF RUNNING

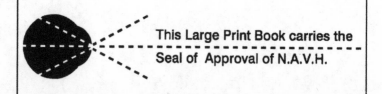

This Large Print Book carries the
Seal of Approval of N.A.V.H.

THE INCOMPLETE BOOK OF RUNNING

PETER SAGAL

THORNDIKE PRESS
A part of Gale, a Cengage Company

Farmington Hills, Mich • San Francisco • New York • Waterville, Maine
Meriden, Conn • Mason, Ohio • Chicago

Copyright © 2018 by Peter Sagal.
Some of the material in this book appeared in different form in *Runner's World* and *AARP The Magazine*.
Thorndike Press, a part of Gale, a Cengage Company.

ALL RIGHTS RESERVED
Thorndike Press® Large Print Lifestyles.
The text of this Large Print edition is unabridged.
Other aspects of the book may vary from the original edition.
Set in 16 pt. Plantin.

LIBRARY OF CONGRESS CIP DATA ON FILE.
CATALOGUING IN PUBLICATION FOR THIS BOOK
IS AVAILABLE FROM THE LIBRARY OF CONGRESS

ISBN-13: 978-1-4328-5683-0 (hardcover)

Published in 2019 by arrangement with Simon & Schuster, Inc.

Printed in Mexico
1 2 3 4 5 6 7 23 22 21 20 19

To my father, who woke me up and said,
"Time to go"

If you can't play sports, run.
If you can't run, run long.

— Author unknown

If you're going through hell, keep going.

— Commonly, and erroneously,
attributed to Winston Churchill

PREFACE

In the midpoint of life, I found myself lost, in a dark place. So I tried to figure out exactly how many miles I had run to get there.

There are obsessive runners who record every fraction of every mile in logbooks piled years-high on their shelves, but I, a distracted, undisciplined person who is lucky if he remembers to write down his name on a check, am not one of them. I've subscribed to various digital services in recent years that supposedly automatically upload all my mileage to websites for the exercise community, but no service will let me use my preferred log-in password, "IFORGOT." So let's try some rough calculation.

I started running at fifteen and pretty soon I was obsessively traversing seven miles of suburban pavement a day, more on the weekends, and I kept that up until the weight loss and hollowed look of my eyes began to freak everyone out, including myself, and then I backed off. So let's say about two thousand miles for my high school career. I jogged sporadically in college when schoolwork or girls or depression or depression about schoolwork and girls didn't get in the way, and they got in the way a lot, so let's just throw on one thousand miles for my entire four years of higher education.

My young adulthood was spent in LA, where sometimes the air was so thick with smog I could imagine seeing the atmospheric particulate matter I had sucked into my lungs coming back out of my nose like a French inhale, so I didn't run much in those five years. Then, like Kurt Russell, I escaped LA and lived out the last of my twenties in Minneapolis, where the air was cleaner but significantly colder, so my running was pretty limited there as well. Let's be conservative and say one thousand miles for the whole decade, bringing us up to four thousand, and let's do the same for my thirties, the years in which I became a parent and got a real job and discovered that telling the mother of my young children that while I completely understood how tired and worn out she was after caring for them all day while I was in the office, I still needed to get a few miles in to improve my mood . . . did not do much for hers. Let's say another thousand for that busy yet indolent decade. As I approached age forty, my guesstimate at my lifelong running odometer stands at five thousand miles.

And then something changed, a change as significant as any other in my life, and perhaps more. Becoming a husband, father, radio host, they all changed my circumstances, significantly and for the better, at least most of the time. But becoming a serious runner at the age of forty, as a way to forestall the mortality that seemed to be (and of course was) closer than it ever had been, changed who and what I am, physically, emotionally, mentally. I went from being a person who ran to being a runner.

How many miles in the thirteen years since then? Fourteen marathons — that's 365 miles right there — plus countless half marathons and ten-mile races and 10Ks and even the occasional 5K, plus miles and miles and miles of training for those races, or doing recovery runs from those races, or just getting out for a run because sitting in the house or office for one second more seemed unbearable.

I have run every single street in my suburb

west of Chicago a thousand times, so much so that if somebody remodels their porch, I notice it. Chicago's Lakefront Trail is a strip of mixed-use recreational pavement that runs for eighteen miles sandwiched between Lakeshore Drive and its namesake, Lake Michigan, and I have run every mile of it so many times that each step of each repetition brings back a specific memory: Here's the stretch where I ran that frozen half marathon in January 2013. Here's where my running buddy Chris and I finished our twenty-mile training run in 2006 in such ragged shape that we told ourselves we'd just try to get to the next lamppost, nothing more ambitious than that, and we counted them out in gasps as we stumbled back to where we parked. Here's the decorative fountain at the midline of the old McCormick Place building that according to Chicago writer Aaron Freeman is the unofficial divider between the northern and southern sections of the path, and thus the divider between White People Exercising and Black People Exercising. Here's Grant Park, where I skittishly started my first-ever marathon in 2005, and thanks to a polygonal but closed-course map, also where I dragged myself over the finish line four hours and three minutes later. There's Navy

Pier, a god-awful yet inexplicably popular tourist attraction, and, because of some terrible sin committed in a prior life, my workplace for twenty years. Let's keep going; I spend too much time there as it is.

And of course I've run in places other than Chicago. Everywhere, in fact. It's been almost fifteen years since I went on a trip without packing my running shoes, shirt, shorts, and socks. On my many trips for *Wait Wait . . . Don't Tell Me!,* the radio show I've hosted since 1998, if I didn't go for a run, I wouldn't have a chance to get out of the hotel or performance space and see where I was. Once, in a city I won't name because I don't want to embarrass Virginia Beach, our hotel was part of the same new mixed-use complex that included our theater. I stepped out of the chain hotel, slowly turned 360 degrees, taking in the Victoria's Secret and the P.F. Chang's and the Auntie Anne's and the generically comfortable and generically welcoming gastropub connected to the generically civic auditorium, and I realized that nothing anywhere in my line of sight gave me a single clue as to where in the United States I might be. So I took off on a run, and ended up in a really shitty part of town next to a rail yard, but at least it was shitty in a charmingly regional way.

Citizens of these United States don't so much travel as we are processed through space, like some sort of industrialized extruded meat product, human Slim Jims. Metal boxes carry us to processing centers that put us on conveyor belts that put us in metal tubes that take us to other processing centers and conveyor belts that put us in different metal boxes that take us to temporary storage cubicles, many of them with lovely minibars for overpriced sustenance. Like hamsters in Habitrails, we think we're free, because that's what the enclosure's designers want us to think. If we didn't do something drastic to punch through the walls, we'd never even know we were trapped.

If visiting a city, I would head for the city center, or if in a state capital, I'd orient toward the building with the golden dome. If in a university town, I'd head for the campus and run on the leafy pathways in the quad, then look for the football stadium, and once there, rattle the door handles. Sometimes I got lucky. Once, at the Yale Bowl in New Haven, I returned a kickoff 110 yards for a touchdown, versus fierce if imaginary opposition.

I have seen remarkable things, and passed them at moderate speed. I have seen sea lions at the end of a deserted pier under the Golden Gate Bridge mating, wrestling, or arguing, or — in the manner of humans — all three at once. I have run up the steps of the Philadelphia Museum of Art just like Rocky and every other middle-aged mook in the world, and I have surprised cows on a country road in New Hampshire and Matthew McConaughey on the path around Town Lake in Austin, Texas (neither mooed). I have come upon, almost as a surprise, the Vietnam Veterans Memorial on the National Mall in Washington, DC, at which point I slowed to a walk and descended into it and emerged at the other end, hoping my bare legs and sweaty shirt would imply no disrespect, and ran off again, feeling newly and powerfully blessed I was able to do so. I have run through arboreal forests in Alaska, along volcanic sand beaches in Hawaii, and because of the fortunate circumstances of my birth, many varied and lovely places in New Jersey.

But I have also ended up in ugly industrial strips, like the one outside Virginia Beach and the one north of Charlotte, North Carolina, and I have become lost in endless, anonymous suburban housing developments, and, in Cobb County, north of Atlanta, a bizarre wasteland of shiny empty office towers next to lonely 1950s-era suburban houses on little islands of lawns, victims of a zoning plan devised by lunatic libertarians. I have passed hulking remnants of the industrial past, like the General Electric plant in Schenectady, New York, and felt an odd reverence, as if visiting a giant tomb. I have conducted running expeditions into my own history, running the three miles from my childhood home to my junior high school — a feat I never could have accomplished when I was required to make that journey every day — and once a six-mile mission to the address of my father's childhood home in Highland Park, Texas, only to find it had been scraped away years prior and replaced by a Greco-columned McMansion. So I just stood in front of the site, put my hand on a tree old enough for my father to have known it, and like he once did, headed off to the northeast at a deliberate pace.

I have stood sweating and panting in front of stores and schools and waterfalls and vistas and garbage dumps. I have run to the tops of hills only to find piled trash and graffiti, or another higher hill beyond, the second in a seemingly infinite rise of obstacles. I have entered the curved streets of new housing developments, like the one I grew up in, and gotten hopelessly lost, as I always worried I would as a child. I have had to end my runs and come back long before I made it anywhere interesting, and I have kept going to get to some fantastic view, only to get back so late I arrived at a cocktail party still sweating into my dress shirt, apologizing to everyone and worrying about the smell.

So: how far is that? We can't waste too much time, we've got a whole book to get through before either of us gets to check Twitter again, so let's just say: twenty thousand miles, for a lifetime total of twenty-five thousand. I have run more than once around the world. And yet, here I still am.

To talk about running is to talk about change and the promise of change. Running, as a topic, has a narcissistic focus on the self — its current flaws and future glories. Unlike every single other amateur sport pursued on the planet, we who do it seldom talk about the people who do it very, very well. Imagine a group of golfers who never talk about professional golfers but maybe had heard of this Tiger Woods fellow only because of that strange thing with his wife and a car crash. Imagine a soccer game in which a player doesn't think of himself as Lionel Messi every time he manages to elude a defender, or a tennis player who slams a winner that skims the net and doesn't say to herself, "Beat that, Serena." But we runners — except for a group of hard-core track nerds — don't know who won the last Berlin Marathon, let alone the American 10,000-meter championship, and we wouldn't recognize the names if we were told them, and we don't really care.* Instead, we talk to ourselves about ourselves and our slow progress.

Every year for the last decade in the United States, some two million people have taken up running, and whether they succeed or don't, they are all looking for the same thing: change. People run from their problems or toward some idealized solution. Running magazines are filled with these uplifting stories, with before and after pictures of people conquering obesity, illness, injury, loss, or grief, with the first picture showing them splaying out of their seat at a dinner table and the second showing them slim and smiling, holding a race finisher's medal.

*In 2017 it was Eliud Kipchoge and Leonard Korir, respectively, which I had to look up just now.

18

The day before the 111th Boston Marathon in 2007, I was invited to participate on a panel of other first-time Boston marathoners by *Runner's World* magazine, for which I soon became a columnist. As we moved down the dais from right to left, each participant told the story of how they conquered whatever obstacles life or overeating or sloth had placed in their way. "I was a fat, unathletic kid," said the first guy, and then the first woman in the group talked about how she conquered both obesity and asthma, and then some guy actually talked about how his cancer — cancer! — had led to the removal of a good part of his brain, and here he was, about to run America's most prestigious and famous marathon. So, that, and yeah, when he was a kid? Fat. Fatty-fat-fat.

I related my own story, which I'll get to later in these pages, but yes, indeed, it did involve my young self waddling around and breathing hard whenever I had to climb some stairs, and then my transformation (skipping a few decades here) into a Boston Marathon qualifier. Finally, the mic was passed to Amy Palmiero-Winters, the world's foremost female below-the-leg-amputee distance runner. She had qualified for Boston (like me, in Chicago the year prior) with a record-setting 3:06 and was looking to run the next day's race in under three hours, the first-ever breaking of the three-hour barrier by any amputee.

Amy took the mic, looked at the rest of us panelists with a subtle but perceptible glance of annoyance, and then turned to the audience.

"Well," she said, "I hate to say it, but I wasn't fat growing up."

"Imagine what you could have accomplished if you were," I said.

Most recreational runners you meet are older, thirty-five and up, leading to the perverse result that it's often easier to win an age-group award in a small race as a younger runner; just recently I almost burst a lung to take third in my age group in my neighborhood 10K with a time that would have won the 25–29 group. This is because most people need a little waft of mortality to motivate them to run seriously, which often means turning thirty, and sometimes, as in my case, forty. I've had, broadly speaking, two running booms in my life — ages fifteen through nineteen or so and ages forty to present — and both of them were inspired by self-loathing and/or an acute awareness of Time's Winged Chariot rushing by. One of the most famous runners in the country, Dean Karnazes, began his career as an ultramarathoner on the night of his thirtieth birthday party, when he became so disgusted with himself he stripped to his shorts, started running down the street, and called his wife the next morning from thirty miles away, asking for a pickup.

So running attracts those in need of change, usually a specific kind of alchemical process by which you can become that which we all want to be: (1) thin, (2) healthy, and thus (3) happy. Running, so simple, so available, seems like a magic trick, and just like at magic shows, people want to be thrilled by miracles.

But in the course of writing this book I went through another kind of transformation. I went from being a married father of three young girls to a divorced father of three teenage girls, and the experience has been about as tumultuous and metamorphic as one of those elaborate charts showing you how oil is refined. I have been through heat and pressure and tight spaces and I have come out annealed into something harder and more brittle than I was.

So because running is life, to write about running is to write about life, and to write about my life is to write about that second transformation as well, into darkness and then back out into the light, at a variable pace.

Traumatic family dramas are the most compelling, time-honored genre of entertainment, from Oedipus to *Desire Under the Elms* to *The Force Awakens.* It is, however, unpleasant to have to live one, so I will not inflict any of the details of my particular crucible on you, dear reader. But at the same time, the story I tell in the book takes place amid events in my personal life that were traumatic, tragic, and sometimes comically surreal. More than once, I woke from a nightmare in my bed to face the same nightmare in waking life. And during all that time I ran, sometimes poorly and slowly, sometimes as if something terrible were chasing me, sometimes feeling more alone than I had ever felt, sometimes as part of a crowd forty thousand strong. Running preserved me, running distracted me, and running prepared me in ways I hadn't anticipated for challenges I couldn't have imagined.

My life changed completely within the space of a single year that started and ended with iterations of the same race. It was the most momentous year of my life, and in many ways the worst, but in retrospect it had to be lived. In the course of telling the story of that single year, I'll have to go back to my childhood, long before I ever imagined I could run farther than the length of a hallway, and I'll imagine the day when something, be it mortality, my failing body, or maybe a wayward truck, stops me in my tracks. There are stories from my long-ago days as a happily married man and from more recent times when I was morally certain I would never be either married or happy again.

Like Kurt Vonnegut's Billy Pilgrim, I am a person unstuck in time. I can be jerked out of the moment completely, by the sight or sound of something that sparks an irresistible memory, or even by my own wandering mind. I can be there talking with you one moment and then I'm a thousand miles and/or ten years away, reliving a particular embarrassment or trauma, or, as is the case more recently, a moment with my children when they were young. Here is the time I crashed a motorcycle. There is the time I toured the Duomo in Florence with my three-year-old daughter, and to keep her from wandering around in the crowd, told her the ceiling had "Papa-attracting paint," and if she let go of my hand, I would float up and away. Here I am thinking of her gripping my hand with both of hers.

And so this story will leap back and forth, following my thoughts where they go, as I relive a year as hard to describe as it was to live through. All told, it is a story of exertion, of learning, of an atrocity that shook the world, and triumphs that mattered only to me, and most of all, a kind of stubborn determination which, as it turns out, is the only athletic skill fate granted to me, other than my aerodynamic skull.

The story ends with me standing on the same patch of ground I'm standing on when it begins, but everything that could be changed had been changed.

ONE

William Greer was seventeen years old when he was riding his bike down the middle of a street in San Antonio, Texas, and was struck by a car. His helmet-less head struck the pavement hard enough to fracture the rear of his skull. His visual cortex was smashed, and although his recovery was miraculous — his father was solemnly told by doctors that William would be institutionalized for the rest of his life — he would never see properly again. His eyes work fine, but his brain can't process the things he sees. Even his wife, Ellen, isn't always sure what he's seeing. I met William on a Sunday, the day before Marathon Monday in Boston, and he and I walked about four city blocks as he narrated his perception: "I see something ahead. It's long, could be a tree. No, it's a pole. A light pole. Okay, we're on the sidewalk . . . up ahead, there's something brown. Is it . . . ?

Okay, a wall."

I asked him about things twenty, thirty feet away. "Do you see the other side of the street? Do you see the doorway to the hotel?"

"No . . . no I don't. Okay, now I think I do. Okay, yes, there's the door, there."

It's easy to think of William's vision as a kind of camera with a very shallow depth of field, so that things float in a blur toward him until they resolve into focus, but that's too mechanical a metaphor for his visual cognition. For William, seeing is often an act of conscious deciphering. For those of us who did not have our skulls slammed into the street at the age of seventeen, this is an automatic act — we see a tree as a tree as easily and unconsciously as blood is pumped from our hearts to our lungs. But William often has to exert conscious effort to constantly piece together an unfamiliar world he is moving through, and he has to do it fast enough to prevent some part of it from leaping up and hurting him.

For William Greer, life is a puzzle he has to figure out every second of his waking life. And standing next to him early the next morning in Hopkinton, Massachusetts, twenty-six point two miles from the intersection of Boylston and Exeter Street in downtown Boston, I knew how he felt.

We had each gotten to Hopkinton by different means and methods. Both of us were in our forties, and both of us had decided to take up serious long-distance running about a decade before. I had run nine previous marathons; William had run six. I was a little faster than he was, but today the plan was to finish at exactly the same time.

William had set his sights on Boston a few years before as many runners do — as his personal Olympics, the one prestigious athletic event that is both selective and attainable. To qualify for Boston, or "run a BQ," as runners often refer to it, is almost every serious marathoner's dream. The qualifying times are graduated by age, making them accessible to, roughly speaking, the top 10 percent of amateur runners of any age group. William, with his disability, needed to run a five-hour marathon to qualify, and he smashed the standard at the prior year's San Francisco Marathon, running it in three hours and fifty-five minutes. Now he had come to Boston to both run the race and to set a new PR, or personal record, with a hoped-for time of three hours and forty-five minutes, which translates to an average pace of eight minutes and thirty-four seconds per mile. Most moderately fit adults would be hard-pressed to run a single mile in that time. William was heading out to do it twenty-six times, and then a few extra hundred yards, for fun. Despite whatever problems he had with his sight, William had boarded the plane to Boston with a clear vision of where he wanted to go, and why, and how quickly.

And me?

On the morning of the marathon, I had arrived in Hopkinton with little planning and less confidence. I didn't exactly know what I was doing there, or what I would do next once I (hopefully) crossed the finish line.

Like William, I had trained and strived and managed to qualify for Boston. But I had done it in the fall of 2006, at my second marathon ever, in Chicago, and I showed up in Boston the next spring only to be nearly drowned as the race was run into the teeth of a freezing rainstorm. When I finished I was so dazed and hypothermic it took as much effort to stagger into the medical tent as it had to run the race. So I requalified in Chicago in 2010 and ran Boston again in 2011, on a perfect day on which an (unofficial) marathon world record was set. Even with blue skies and a following breeze it's still a tough race, and as I stumbled through the finishing chute on Boylston Street, with a satisfying if not record-setting time of 3:27, I said to myself, and to anyone who would listen, that I had no reason to run Boston ever again.

Yet here I was.

I came back to run Boston in 2013 because, like Lolita, you see, I had absolutely nowhere else to go. My strained, trembling marriage of nineteen years had finally shaken itself to pieces. Since our agreement to divorce three months earlier, my wife and I had settled into a cold war that occasionally flashed hot as it became clear that it would not be and could never have been the amicable split I had hoped for, for our sake and for that of our three daughters. Instead of a "conscious uncoupling," it was turning into a brush war, fought out in our hundred-year-old Victorian house west of Chicago, a four-story maze of minefields and trip wires.

I started accepting many of the invitations that came my way, anything to get me out of the house and removed from the battlefield. I hosted a few fund-raisers, spoke at a few events. And when a contagiously enthusiastic young man named Josh Warren called and offered me the chance to run Boston a third time, this time as a guide for a blind runner, I said, "Sure." What the hell, I told myself, at least somebody wanted to see me. Even if he was blind. Maybe because he was blind.

My future was uncertain to the point of being a blank. I didn't know where I would live, or whom I might live with. I didn't know if I'd be alone for the rest of my life. At the age of forty-eight, everything I had accomplished in my personal life — my marriage, my three children, my home — was slipping away from me. What was left? Well, I had trained myself to run marathons. That's a thing! So I volunteered to run a marathon for someone else, just because Josh asked me. It had never occurred to me before then that this solipsistic activity could be of use to someone else, beyond, say, pulling his sled across the tundra.

Race day: at 5 AM I met Josh, William, and the other runners and guides of Team With A Vision at a downtown Boston hotel, where we got into the rented bus and headed out to Hopkinton. Boston is unlike most other modern urban marathons, which tend to start and finish at the same place. The Boston Marathon, born in a simpler and more honest age, starts twenty-six miles due west of where it ends. You begin your day in downtown Boston near the finish line, then you get on a bus that drives you every foot of the distance of the course, and then the bastards expect you to run back.

After forty minutes on the road the bus stopped a block away from the marathon start line at the Hopkinton Vision Center, an optician's office which had been donated to Team With A Vision as a staging base. It was filled with runners and their guides eating energy bars and bagels, drinking coffee and Gatorade, and using and reusing the two bathrooms. We arrived more than three hours before our third-wave start of 10:15 AM, so some of us napped. I caught a few winks in an optician's exam chair, snoring into the phoropter.

Before our start, William and I posed for a photo with Josh Warren and his wife, Lisa, outside the vision center. Lisa is a petite woman, about five feet tall, the same height as my oldest daughter, who was fifteen at the time. As I looked at her, I was struck by a pang of loneliness and loss, a stark reminder that I was here looking after William because at the moment I wasn't able to look after anybody else. Before I allowed myself to think about how weird it would be to actually do this — I'd met her that very morning! — I asked Lisa if I could pick her up. She laughed and said yes. I picked up Lisa, and then we all held her across our line of men, like she was a bathing beauty on the Atlantic City boardwalk, or maybe like a giant fish we had all just caught.

I stood there smiling for the camera and thought about my daughters, who, when they were very young, I used to pick up, put on my shoulders, and loudly ask, "Where did she GO?" And my girls would shriek and laugh and say, "I'm up HERE, Papa!" and I would say, "I can hear her voice, but where is she?" and there would be more laughter, and I would run around the room looking just everywhere until finally I came to a mirror and discovered the amazing truth.

After the photo was taken — it ended up going around on Twitter, and my quadriceps came in for some admiration — and the Gatorade was drunk, the energy bars were eaten, the Body Glide was applied, bibs were carefully pinned and repinned, and the bathrooms were again used and reused, William and I walked toward the starting line. We were in the third of three start waves; each of them contained more than ten thousand runners. Our wave was primarily charity runners — runners who had pledged to raise a certain amount for one of the approved marathon charities, and thus hadn't had to run a certain time to qualify for the race. At my prior Bostons, I had started in the first and second waves, and as I looked around I noticed a much more eclectic group than the mostly male, mostly skinny, mostly jackal-eyed runners I usually began with. Here in the third wave, there were people of all shapes and all ages, and instead of the predatory demeanor of my usual crowd, they all looked a little happy and a little nervous, like they were about to go on a particularly scary roller coaster. Many of them had written their names in large letters on their shirts to attract personalized cheers, and many of them had written their purposes as well, or had them preprinted: FOR MARY . . . NO MORE HUNGER . . . RUN FOR A CURE. During the course of the race, those runners would be engaged in an alphanumeric conversation with the amusing signs held aloft by spectators: ONLY TEN MILES TILL BEER . . . DON'T TRUST A FART FROM HERE ON OUT.

William was nervous, I think; it's hard to tell someone is anxious if he never looks you in the eye to begin with. All marathons are a little intimidating, but few of them begin so mysteriously as Boston. The Chicago Marathon starts on the city's front porch in Grant Park, and you know you will return to that point; the Philadelphia Marathon similarly starts and finishes in front of the Philadelphia Museum of Art, where Rocky ran the steps. From the Verrazano-Narrows Bridge, where the New York City Marathon begins, you can see Manhattan, where the race ends. But the Boston Marathon starts in a small town on a road that leads downhill into the woods and then vanishes. There is no view, no hint of what is to come. For Boston rookies — for me, back in 2007 — the sheer anxiety of it can approach the terror of stepping off a ladder into darkness. There is no inkling of where you will land, or how much it will hurt.

We were the last segment in the elongated body of runners, the abdomen in the tripartite multilegged beast. A major marathon is the only sporting event in which an amateur who pays the fee (and, in Boston's case, qualifies or gets a charity bib) can compete against the best athletes in the world. You can't pay a hundred and fifty bucks and enter Wimbledon. But you can stand behind the same starting line as the finest marathoners in the world: skinny, compact men and women, (mostly) with ebony skin and a loose loping pace that looks relaxed even when churning out 4:30 miles. It's scientifically possible you could beat them, in exactly the same way it's scientifically possible that all the atoms in your body could align perfectly with the gaps between the atoms in the wall in front of you and you could run right through it.

Of course, it almost never happens that any amateur actually beats an elite professional runner. In 2008, an amateur entrant named Arien O'Connell ran a 2:55:11 at the Nike Women's Marathon in San Francisco, beating out all three of the top elite runners, but the race organizers refused to honor her win. They claimed her time didn't count, because while her elapsed time beat theirs, they had finished first. Of course they had — the elite runners were given a twenty-minute head start on the rest of the field. The real reason, everyone presumed, is that the elite runners are paid to appear, and paid to win. She was not. After a public outcry in the running community, O'Connell was awarded a co–first place medal. And more recently, in a repeat of the cold and wet conditions that I endured in 2007, a nurse anesthetist named Sarah Sellers took second place at the 2018 Boston Marathon, passing dozens of elites who probably thought they weren't being paid enough to feel that miserable.

If William and I were going to perform that kind of miracle, we'd best be quick about it. The leaders were at that moment more than halfway down the course, sprint-loping toward winning times in two hours and a fraction. Catching them would be, shall we say, unlikely, but one of the great and terrifying things about marathon running is that there really is no predicting the future. Nobody dares to call their shot if that shot is supposed to land twenty-six miles away. Marathoning is probably closer to mountain climbing than to any other sport. You prepare for months, you practice and train, but then comes the day with the challenge before you, and you realize that the result will depend on the wind, the temperature, what you chose to eat the night before, what you chose not to eat, not to mention the cooperation of your gut, lungs, heart, and legs. You can train all you want, but twenty-six miles is too great a length to allow for any confidence in the outcome. Sometimes, as with Boston in 2018, miracles occur, as one did for Sellers. Or disaster strikes, as it did with hometown hero Shalane Flanagan in the same race. Flanagan had won the New York City Marathon just six months earlier, but in Boston she ended up stumbling into a porta-potty as the rest of the field streamed ahead of her.

Ten thirty AM. For the third time that morning, the PA system played the national anthem, and for the third time that morning, nine thousand regimented runners removed their caps and placed their hands over the technical fabric covering their muscular hearts. For the third time that morning, the starter intoned "On your marks . . . set . . . go!" The lock and dam at Hopkinton Town Common swung open, and a wave of runners burst onto Route 135 heading east.

The first mile of any marathon goes by in a painless blur. Anybody, no matter how out of shape, could run a mile if it was the first one in a mass urban marathon — it provides all the adrenaline of running with a mob, albeit without the heretics in front or giant monsters behind. People cheer and whoop and run much faster than they should, with some — okay, many — okay, me — immediately starting to dodge and dart around and ahead of other runners. Because at that moment, as your legs start to move after what seems like hours of jumping in place, you feel infinitely energetic, like you will own this day, and despite any lack of, say, appropriate training or nutrition or any right to be attempting this, you will easily compact the physical reality between you and the finish line, and via a kind of warp drive, sprint to the end. It doesn't last long, this feeling of elation, but still there is no better feeling than starting a marathon. It beats finishing one with a hammer.

William and I dodged around runners, with me trying to guard him from interference. Per his instructions, I was supposed to run slightly ahead of William and to his left, where his field of vision was clearest, but at the start of the race, I thought it was more important to stay straight in front of him like a shield. I was leading William as a herald, letting runners know that a blind runner was coming up behind them. I shouted "Excuse me!" and the runners turned in annoyance, and I got to enjoy watching their faces as they registered the GUIDE bib I was wearing and the BLIND RUNNER bib on William. "Oh!" they'd said as they bowed to my superior virtue and got out of the way.

Whenever the crowds in front cleared, I shifted to lagging behind William to protect him from runners overtaking from the rear. That didn't make a lot of sense, in that the runners overtaking us were not blind themselves and wouldn't be madly charging into a runner in front of them, but it seemed noble in a kind of jumping-on-the-grenade way, so I did it.

However, my principal responsibility, as William had laid it out the day prior, was to warn him of turns in the course, as well as obstacles in the roadway. As a blind runner, William's greatest fear was stepping into a pothole or tripping over a streetcar track embedded in the pavement. Unlike a sighted person, he couldn't even prepare himself for the impact if he did trip — the first evidence he'd have of a mishap (as he knew from experience) would be the pain as he struck the pavement. So I was to shout out warnings.

So I scanned the course, which had been cleared, repaired, checked, rechecked, and then polished just that morning by the thousands of runners in front of us, and since there were no holes to dodge, and two entire real turns on the whole course, both of them in the last mile, there wasn't much to distract us, other than the fact that we were running a marathon. William and I just talked. We talked pace — to complete his marathon on time, he needed to maintain an even 8:34 pace per mile, but Boston's course is anything but even. It begins with a steady, sometimes even steep descent, then is fairly flat through the towns of Ashland, Framingham, and Natick, then through Wellesley — the town and campus — and of course then come the famous Newton Hills, four of them, culminating with the famous Heartbreak Hill that crests at Boston College, with the first sight of downtown Boston in the distance. Those hills are not particularly steep, but they come at exactly the wrong time, starting in mile 17, when most marathoners start to flag and fail anyway. First-time Boston marathoners go out too fast at the beginning, whooping and leaping in the excitement of starting the Greatest Race in the World, and then they get to the tough part and they realize that they were completely unprepared and stupid to even attempt it. It's a lot like marriage.

There are, broadly speaking, two ways to approach marathoning. The first is tactical. You plan your race, sketch out goal splits for each mile, plot when to take nutrition and when to take fluids and when to press and when to lay back and when to finally kick to the finish. This is a somewhat military approach, and in practice it has worked out about as well for me as it did for the World War I British generals planning out their attack on the Ypres Salient. And so I have come slowly to another view, based on longtime experience and disappointment. I now believe, along with Sun Tzu, that the war is lost or won long before the day of battle. You train, mentally and physically, as best you can, and on the day of the race you cast yourself upon the road and see where your legs can take you. You run until somebody or something tells you to stop.

Today, for this marathon, I was supposed to help William get to where he wanted — the finish line — by the time he wanted to get there. I was worried I would screw it up. My nightmare for the day was William standing, frustrated, by the side of the road as I vomited or helplessly emitted something even less pleasant. I was at a moment in my life when I had disappointed just about everyone who claimed some duty from me. I wasn't going to do it again. Not today. At least not for the next three hours and forty-five minutes, or so we hoped.

We ran, and we talked more. William has the flat affect you sometimes find in people with neurological injuries, which, along with his sidelong glance, gives him an air of distraction, as if he is always thinking of something more interesting than he could share. But his wandering look was a thin shroud over his intelligence and humor. He

41

liked my radio show and had many questions about it, particularly his favorite guest we've ever featured: the writer Carl Hiaasen. I told him some stories about Carl, and we cruised through miles five, six, and seven.

Eventually we got to talking about my own life and what had brought me to this moment. I told him about my increasingly difficult marriage and its demise. It's an odd thing to tell your troubles to a person with much worse troubles, especially if he would not agree with that comparison. William Greer is an ambulatory self-pity suppressor zone.

The first half of the race sped by beautifully, as it often does at Boston. You descend gradually through the wooded roads of Hopkinton and Ashland and you settle into a groove — sometimes literally, if you don't watch for the train tracks — as you run through the more built-up suburbs of Framingham and Natick. Early on, the crowds are sporadic, often gathered in front of restaurants and cafes, some of them apparently getting an early start on honoring the patriots of Patriots' Day by binge drinking, as our founding fathers did, probably. The crowds were thickest at each town center, and as we ran by, children would come to the forefront of the crowds and stick out their hands for sweaty high fives.

I've watched a few marathons, including back when I never had any thought of running one myself. In the crowd, there's a growing anticipation as the leaders approach, preceded like dignitaries by waves of police cars, police motorcycles, and TV trucks. The elites come speeding by, their faces blank, and you applaud, and then you can cheer for the other elites — ones who have won races but won't today — as everyone gets excited for the first woman, who is often met by cries of "First woman!" (Pro tip: she knows.) And then the crowds shout for the next few women, or perhaps a local or nationally ranked runner who's doomed to finish thirty or forty places behind the leaders today, still an amazing athletic performance, one that won't rescue him or her from obscurity but might earn a small sponsorship or an appearance fee at a smaller race.

And then, like the flowing sheets of snow that follow the first bouncing snowballs of an avalanche, they come: the hundreds and then thousands of runners, crowded among one another. Their shapes gradually but visibly change from razor-thin to short, tall, bulbous, top-heavy, and bottom-heavy. It's not quite a parade, not a panicked flight, not a mass migration, and not really a race between competitors, but it has qualities of all of them. It is a joyful, colorful, intense, grim, and sometimes unpleasant sight, depending on who you happen to see, where you're seeing them, and how they're feeling. If you're watching at the eighteenth mile or farther on, you'll see people walking, fading to the side of the road, grabbing at their calves, knees, or the ground itself. Stephen King once wrote a novel called *The Long Walk* in which young men have to complete a long-distance endurance walk, with the stragglers shot by guards. I assume he conceived of this story while watching the latter portion of a marathon field in the latter part of the course.

Still, this was the early going, and so William and I cruised by the pubs and train stations of the western Boston suburbs happily and easily, along with thousands of other happy runners. The marathon had been underway for hours, and the crowds might have just arrived, or they might have been there all day. I appreciated their durability, and I understood it. When you're standing there watching a race, you're always tempted to walk away, back to your life, back to your job, but you always stay to wave at one more smiling face, one more sweaty brow. And you cheer. There's something very pleasing about expressing unbridled enthusiasm, and the sidelines of a marathon are one of the few places on the public streets you can do it, unless your local team wins a championship, your kid is in the Fourth of July parade, or the allied forces have just liberated your city from the occupiers.

Once we left behind the crowds in downtown Wellesley, and ran over the stripe marking the halfway point at mile 13.1, we entered a grove of trees, with few if any spectators, and from far ahead of us came a strange, high-pitched roar, which started out like the sound of an ocean in the distance and then resolved into human voices, limited to a narrow, high range of frequency. I grinned, and I promised William, "You're going to like this."

It was the Wellesley Scream Tunnel, one of the great traditions of the Boston Marathon. The course cuts right through the Wellesley campus, and for decades, the Wellesley students have lined a barrier on the side of the course, erected specifically to keep them from overwhelming the runners. They are engaged in some sort of competition — informal or regimented, I never found out — to gather the most kisses from

45

runners, so the girls all wave signs reading KISS ME! or KISS ME! I'M A HISTORY MAJOR or GAY/JEWISH/FROM CALIFORNIA, hoping to strike a chord in someone similarly situated. To use a few words freighted in both kissing and running circles, I thought William would make out like a bandit. He's a blind runner! A hero, triumphing over his adversity! They'd be all over him! And me, his helpful guide, well, certainly my charity would earn me similar plaudits. If I had brought breath freshener, now would be the time to whip it out for a few puffs.

To my dismay, William steered himself away from the shrieking women on his right, deigning to extend a warm hand to slap some offered in return. He was treating the Scream Tunnel like a nineteenth-century European courting ritual, careful to maintain a modest distance between himself and the single ladies. "What are you doing?" I actually yelled.

"I promised Ellen," William yelled back to me, "that I would never kiss anybody but her!"

"She'll never know!" I yelled back.

"I would!" he said, and ran right past the last screaming girl with a wave. I stopped and kissed one at random on the cheek, grinned guiltily, and sprinted off after William. It was the first time I had kissed anyone since New Year's Eve, when my wife and I had exchanged our last kiss ever, a dry peck that sealed off the prior two decades of our lives from whatever was next.

Things began to go south for William as we continued to make our way east, the screams from the Wellesley women fading in the background. He told me he needed a porta-potty, so I found him one at the next water stop. Then again a mile later. Then again a mile later. As I stood outside the plastic shacks, waiting for William to re-emerge, watching the minutes tick away, I was only grateful that it wasn't me in there. If anybody's bowels were going to cost William his goal, let them not be mine.

William cruised up and past the Route 128 overpass, a kind of warm-up for the real hills to come, and then he conquered the first of the true Newton Hills, Firehouse Hill, with a focus and pace that made me think he was going to handle all of them with ease. But Firehouse and the next hill took a lot out of him, and we weren't two hundred yards up the third hill before he asked to walk for the first time. The longer you walk in a running race, the harder it is to get going again. The muscles start to cool and seize and as the exhaustion and pain fade it becomes that much harder to motivate yourself to start running and suffering again. I tried to push William, as I knew he had lost the chance to make his 3:45 PR, but he might still have a chance to hit a sub-3:50, and certainly, with a sustained effort, he could come in under four hours, which was his absolute standard, he had told me, for an acceptable race.

But the day was rolling on, and we were slowing down, and then we came to Heartbreak.

The name "Heartbreak Hill" became attached to this particular upward slope of Commonwealth Avenue because of the famous iteration of the race back in 1936, when an upstart delightfully named Tarzan Brown managed to blow past perennial champion Johnny Kelley right at that final hill, "breaking Kelley's heart" as Brown went forward to the win. But over the years the name has come to define the hill as modern running's most famous peril, the Minotaur of marathoning. If you are an amateur marathoner, then the mild hills of Newton — none of them, not even Heartbreak, are the kind of hill you'd even notice if you were driving up it while listening to a particularly good podcast — come at exactly the wrong time, miles 17 through 21, the part of a marathon known as "the wall," when your inner physical and mental reserves are depleted and the last thing in the world you want to see, with apologies to the plaque hanging in every Irish bar, is the road rising up to meet you.

Now, in addition to his stomach cramps, William had cramps in his left leg, and we had to stop to try to stretch it out. I watched him nervously. I had told him I would turn off my running watch and we'd forget about the elapsed time, but I was too invested in his success to actually do it. Besides, what was he going to do? See it?

As for me, I felt fine. Better than fine. I had suffered through various marathons to various degrees; on my first Boston, in 2007, I had felt as bad as he did right now, for similar reasons. I remember giving everything I had to get to the top of Heartbreak, realizing I still had five miles yet to go, and practically weeping with misery. But this time, as focused as I was on William, his gut, his leg, his loyalty to his wife (damn him), and his race, I hadn't even noticed my own fatigue. We stopped to walk part of the way up Heartbreak, to give his aching body a rest, but still I felt strangely fine: I was twenty miles into a marathon and all I could think about was figuring out a way to get us both running again.

William made it to the top, exhausted and in pain, and for a reward we got a lovely vista of the five miles we had left to go before the finish. William stopped again and stretched out his cramping leg against a light pole in front of Boston College, where the students had come out en masse to cheer. One young woman shouted "Good job!" at William. He shook his head grimly, not agreeing at all, but I engaged her in conversation. Turns out Jess was a junior at BC and had run the marathon herself. "What are you doing on that side of the barrier?" I asked. She shrugged, laughing. "Well, come on, then! Run with us!" She and her friend, both wearing jeans, sneakers, and light jackets, crossed the barrier and the four of us ran together. I made sure they flanked William as we ran down the slope of Commonwealth Avenue heading into Boston proper, and blind or not, Ellen or not, I noticed him picking up his head and his legs and feigning confidence. The sight of a pretty girl has a powerful effect, even on the sightless. (For the record, William denies that their being attractive had anything to do with it; he just enjoyed the company of someone else to run with for a bit. Hello, Ellen!)

But Jess and her friend weren't dressed or prepared to run, and each step was taking them farther from their friends in the company of an odd-looking man and his squat, bald companion, so they stopped and wished us luck and headed back after about a half mile, and soon William asked to stop and walk again. I could see that he was frustrated, but the pain was greater than the frustration, so we stopped. I tried to motivate him by how close we were to the finish: "Do you see the Prudential building, William? It's about four miles away."

"No."

"How about that big building up ahead? Can you see that? Maybe we can try running to it before our next break."

"I can't see it."

It was only about four hundred yards ahead. We continued to walk.

"My parents and my uncle and aunt are going to be waiting for us near mile 23," I said. "Let's make sure we're running when we get there, okay? I want to impress them."

I surreptitiously looked at my running watch. Unless we started running consistently, we would not make it under four hours. In fact, we were looking at a 4:10 finish, unless William collapsed completely, which seemed possible. But he managed to pull it together enough to run by my family as my aunt snapped a picture:

William had the courtesy to run another few hundred yards beyond them before walking again. He was in pain, and I was in a bind. I wanted William to run. I had adopted his goal as my own, and it had become extremely important to me — as a runner, as a person, as a guide, as a caretaker in need of someone to take care of — to get William to that line in under four hours. I might have wanted it more than William did, and I found myself getting almost angry at him for flagging. Next thing you knew, I'd be docking his allowance.

But at the same time, I was there to be of service to him, to help him run his race, whatever the outcome might be. If he wanted to walk, we would walk. If he wanted to stop and get a cheeseburger and a smoke, we would do that. Still, I couldn't help trying to nudge him one last time. "William," I said, "I know you're not feeling your best, but you just can't walk the last mile of the Boston Marathon. You make a right turn onto Hereford Street, and then a left onto Boylston, and then, there you are, on the last quarter mile of the race, the tall buildings around you, the crowds six deep and shouting. It's like your own ticker-tape parade."

William took it in but didn't respond.

We passed the mile-25 marker — one mile and change to go. William started running. I could practically hear him gritting his teeth with the effort required.

"Where's that first right turn?" he asked.

"About two hundred yards ahead," I said.

"I'm going to have to walk when we get there," he replied.

Okay. So be it. My watch read a minute or two over four hours. William had blown it, or maybe I had. Walking now wouldn't matter; he had missed his final goal. The race was a failure, or at least, it seemed, I was.

But when we got to that right turn onto

Hereford Street, William didn't start walking. He accelerated. I was to his left, in my appointed place. He turned right and sped up. No words had passed between us. He ran hard, going ahead of me — straight toward a pothole, marked by a dented yellow traffic cone.

In the entire marathon course, almost all twenty-six miles to this point, there had not been a single obstacle in the course or a significant flaw in the roadway, and now William was running directly toward the very first one. I had just enough time to register its presence — it was marking a hole that must have materialized on race morning — and I started to shout "Watch out for the —" but then William, suddenly gifted with the sight and reflexes of a ninja, deftly dodged around it. And kept going.

I managed to catch up with him as we turned left onto Boylston Street, but then I intentionally fell behind a step. He didn't need my guidance anymore.

"Three hundred yards!" I shouted to William. He picked up his pace.

"Two hundred yards!" I shouted.

Boylston Street is lined with stores and bars, and it is a popular place to watch the marathon. You get to cheer the runners through their last happy sprints for the finish. On cold Patriots' Days, the shops — such as Marathon Sports, located right before the finish line — provide warmth when you need it, so they're a particularly good spot for spectators with small children. It can be extremely crowded, but as the winners and other elites had long since crossed the line — most of them were already showered and dressed and enjoying their well-earned lunch — and the finishers were now all charity runners and slowpoke civilians, just about anybody who liked could walk up and join the throng on the sidewalks on Boylston Street.

The people cheered and clapped. I waved my arms for even more cheering and clapping. "His name is William!" I yelled.

"Go, William!" yelled the crowd.

"The finish line is right there!" I shouted to William. I was shouting everything. If my daughters were there, I would have shouted "I LOVE YOU!" into their faces. "Can you see it, William? Can you see it?"

"I can see it!"

William Greer crossed the finish line of the Boston Marathon and kept running.

I said, "You made it! You can stop!" William stopped. I hugged his sweaty, trembling form, grinning like an idiot. "You did it! You did it!" I was as proud of him as I'd ever been of anyone in my life. By his own standards, William had failed. He hadn't set a new PR, hadn't finished in under four hours . . . by the goals he had laid out before we started, it was one of the worst marathons he'd ever run, and he was exhausted. I didn't care. To me, he had won the damn thing, and the moment lacked only a laurel wreath to crown him.

The adrenaline drained quickly from both of us, and seconds after his last sprint, William was now doubled over, struggling to breathe. A medic, on the watch for runners in distress, approached and asked if he needed help. William politely declined and kept trying to slow his breathing. About five minutes had passed since we had crossed the line, but we hadn't moved more than a hundred yards away into the finishers' chute, the long longitudinal area manned by volunteers, security officers, and medics, and stocked with boxes of medals, blankets, and refreshments for the triumphant runners.

All William's heroic dash had really done, from a clinical perspective, was shave five minutes off what would have been our final time. We had crossed the line in 4:03. The clock above the line now read 4:09. If he had walked that last mile, as he had intended to (and probably believed he would until the moment he refused to do it), we would most likely still have been on the course, approaching the line just then. A woman passed me on my left, one of the many exhausted runners streaming around us, as we started to finally walk away from the line, farther into the chute and toward its rewards.

There was a very loud noise.

TWO

I'm watching my father in the basement, jumping up and down and waving his arms. I am about six, and he is too old for this nonsense. Propped open on the otherwise unused wet bar is a Royal Canadian Air Force exercise guide, inexplicably but widely popular in the late 1960s, instructing him to stretch and leap and reach for his toes, and then, finally, to jog in place, perambulating about the basement, his legs churning disproportionately compared to the good it seems to do him. Nonetheless, this is the first time I can remember seeing my father run.

My father was born in Brooklyn in 1936 as Matthew Malkin, and he spent his childhood there, in a time and place where the only people running on the street were either chasing someone or being chased. "Physical culture" was then popular only with soldiers, health fetishists, and closeted homosexuals. He was raised by a single mother, as his father, my biological grandfather Simon Malkin, had run off with a younger woman when little Matty was but one year old, completely and permanently abandoning both him and his ten-year-old brother, Robert. My father's mother, Helen Malkin (née Kirschenbaum), thus became one of those rare and shameful things in respectable if poor Brooklyn Jewish circles: a single mother. "A shandah," they would have whispered. "What's wrong with her?"

When Matty was twelve or so, my grandmother came home and announced that he should dress nicely, because he was to meet someone, a special someone, and that he was to address this new gentleman, upon meeting him, as "Dad." The marriage to Mark Sagal — a fortyish bachelor who did not have and perhaps did not want any children — soon followed, as did formal adoption of Helen's son. Matty (now) Sagal duly followed his new dad and his old mom out to Mark Sagal's new job in Highland Park, Texas, a suburb of Dallas filled with prosperous oilmen, their pleasantly dutiful wives, and their "colored help." For a Jewish kid from Brooklyn, it must have been as alien as Ouagadougou. Decades later, after my grandpa's death, I learned that this and other moves in his life might have had something to do with his unreliability as an engineer, which might have had something to do with his reliability as a drinker of the scotch and waters that, later on in the 1970s, I would watch him and my father stir and sip in Grandpa and Grandma's apartment on the Upper East Side of Manhattan.

I've looked through my father's yearbook from Highland Park High. There are the tall, handsome/pretty blond Texans on the football and baseball and cheerleading squads, and there is Matty Sagal, with his shiny black hair and horn-rimmed glasses, in the school play, on the masthead of the school paper. If during that time in his life my father ever moved for pleasure, for exercise, or for competition, there is no photographic record of it. Off he went to college to study engineering, as his stepfather demanded, and then to graduate school, and then to marriage, and then, as one did then, to choose between two or three competing offers from large corporations, each promising full employment until a pensioned retirement and a comfortable death.

The choice made (Bell Laboratories), he and his wife, my mother, Reeva Sagal (née

Scholnick), duly moved to New Jersey, and duly reproduced: first Doug, born in 1962, then myself in 1965, and then our brother, Roger, in 1970. By the time the day of that basement memory came around, Matty — now Matthew W. Sagal on his business cards, Matt to his friends, and Matt the Rat to his enemies in office politics — was a suburban dad — such as I was to become — working for a single employer that provided him security and income stability such that his children wouldn't be suddenly jerked across the country due to the whims of their parents' failures in marriage or employment or sobriety. He must have felt, as I did when I arrived at that age and station some decades later, that he was getting older before his time, that — like the astronaut in the final sequence of *2001: A Space Odyssey* — he could look across the room and see the old man he was going to become, huddled over a soup dish, or tucked into a bed with the covers up to his chin, laboring to breathe. He decided to get some exercise.

Thus, there he was in the basement, jogging in place, trying to get his knees as high as he could, occasionally waving his arms up above his head in the manner of a jumping jack. I remember him puffing his breath out and in through pursed lips, like a fish, his bald head beaded with sweat. "What an idiot," I thought to myself.

From that day onward, riding the pressure wave of the 1970s running boom, he continued to run like an idiot all over suburban New Jersey, sometimes with me watching — on one disastrous occasion, with me following along in a community 10K on my banana seat bike — but eventually with me openly mocking. I protected my pudgy, uneasy, unattractive self with a layer of sarcasm that thickened as I approached adolescence, and I gave my father more than his fair share of it. "Funny, Dad, you ran six miles; I stayed here eating frozen waffles, and lookie here: we both ended up in the same place!" He didn't react to these provocations. He just snorted a bit and shook his head and went to shower.

But secretly, I envied him. Like just about everyone in that time and place and demographic, my father had purchased a copy of Jim Fixx's *The Complete Book of Running*, the Koran of the 1970s running boom. I would leaf through it sometimes, when nobody was around, and for a slow, unathletic kid like me, it was a kind of porn.

I admired the photograph of the author's lower half on the cover: the right leg, in the background, tucked up toward the shorts, the foot blurred in motion as it finished its upward arc, and then the left leg in mid-stride, pushing off the ball of an Onitsuka Tiger racing flat, the whole photo a Michelangelo masterpiece of delineated muscle. I would look at my doughy thighs, stretch them out, and search for any hint of muscle within. It was like looking for a needle in a stack of Jell-O.

The legs remain, I am happy to report, on the cover of the copy Jim Fixx's son sent me after I wrote about the book for *Runner's World.* On the back flap, the author comes running straight at you as if he can't wait to give you the good news. Like all of history's greatest evangelists — e.g., Saul of Tarsus — Fixx was a convert. "When he started running several years ago," the flap copy reads, "Jim Fixx weighed nearly 220 pounds and breathed hard just thinking about exercise. Today, at 159 pounds, he has been declared medically fitter than most college athletes . . . and has run the equivalent of once around the equator."

The book is just as I remember it. There are those particularly mid-70sish black ink drawings, strangely and uncomfortably like the ones in *The Joy of Sex* (which my father didn't have on his shelf, at least not that shelf). All the runners pictured are skinny guys with sideburns and girls with ponytails, in cotton T-shirts and blissed-out faces. And then there is the heart of the book: the promises.

Fixx didn't call them that, of course, but to me that's what they were: Promises of what would happen if you — if I — could only run. Running will make you healthy and slender, a cure for almost any modern illness (chapter 1), happier and more peaceful (chapter 2), and you'll be able to enjoy this peaceful, happy life long into old age (chapter 4). To do it, all you need is a pair of good running shoes, for which you should be willing to spend "as much as $20 to $40," and shorts. Period. Fixx reserved his only doubt about running for shirts and socks. He wasn't sure you needed either. (Pro tip: socks are good.)

I turn to my favorite chapter — chapter 14, "Eat to Run: Good News If You Really Love Food." I did and do love food, and back then food was the only one of my many growing appetites I could practically indulge, so I was in dire need of some good news. I used to read that chapter over and over, gazing at the ink drawing of the huge plate of spaghetti and meatballs. Fixx praises the then-new idea of carbo-loading, and even though I had yet to run a step, or ever imagined that I could, I had a head start on that art. To be able to eat what I wanted, and not feel sick or guilty or as if I were swelling like a balloon! The impact of this pretty simple book, so low-key by the standards of today's glossy fitness bibles with their lurid color photos of the fantastically fit celebrity trainer on the cover, is hard to overstate. The book had thirty printings in its first two years and sold more than a million copies internationally — those figures coming from the foreword to *Jim Fixx's Second Book of Running,* which Fixx published (somewhat sheepishly) as a sequel to *The Complete Book of Running* three years later, in 1980. But the more impressive figures are those describing the running boom itself. He estimates the number of runners in the United States as growing from six million when he sat down to write the first book, to twenty-five million as he published the second — a fourfold increase in just a few years.

This was the era of jogging suits and headbands, with the rise of Nike and the making of Michael Douglas's most obscure movie, *Running,* in which the addicted hero starts the film putting on suit and tie and sneakers, then begins to run, and is soon sprinting across the Queensboro Bridge to pick up his daughter from his estranged ex-wife, with his tie wrapped around his forehead in lieu of a sweatband, as one does. When I saw that movie on TV one night in 1980, I couldn't imagine doing any of those things.

As for Fixx, he went from being an obscure author of intellectual puzzle books to a wealthy, bestselling one, and a national and international celebrity doing the talk show circuit, appearing in ads for American Express ("Do you know me?") and Quaker Oats, but not, despite a lucrative offer, Budweiser.

"He loved beer," his friend Buzz McCoy told me. "But he just didn't think it was appropriate for a fitness advocate to advertise it."

McCoy met Fixx on the streets and trails of suburban Connecticut, where they both lived and ran in the 70s. He says Fixx was a social runner, talented but never intensely competitive, the kind of man who would jog in the last few miles of a race with a friend rather than blazing ahead to get a better time. It was his lack of ego, McCoy believes, that made his book so successful.

"His personality, his unassuming nature, and his modesty — it made running not a he-man thing, but something for forty-year-old divorced women, and young women, and people who had beer bellies, people who couldn't walk in a straight line. It opened it up to them."

And, I could have added, it opened it up to "husky" teenagers in suburban New Jersey.

In 1984, Fixx died at the age of fifty-two — satisfactorily and distantly old to me when it happened, now about my age as I write — of a massive heart attack suffered while on his daily ten-mile run. He was found, true to his creed, by the side of a country road, shirtless, in just shoes and shorts. There were those who cried, "Ha! Running will kill you!" Others pointed out that Fixx had inherited the same congenital heart defect that killed his father at an even younger age. Some pointed their fingers at Fixx's dismissal of good nutrition — maybe runners can't, or at least shouldn't, eat anything they liked. But it was probably mostly this: Buzz McCoy remembers that for all of his friend's obsession with running as a pathway to health, Fixx himself never saw, or even knew, a doctor.

Back in 1980, all that was yet to come. But on a certain evening in the spring of that year, when I was fifteen, I shuffled over to my father, my eyes fixed on the shag carpet, and asked him if I could get up with him the next morning to go running. He didn't say any of the things that I expected to hear, like, "What? All this time you've been making fun of me, and now you want to come along? Guess you feel like looking like an idiot too, huh?" He just said, "Sure. I'll wake you up at six." And he did, too, damn him.

What had changed my mind about running? Well, at some point around that time, I had become painfully aware that I put most of my physical self, the five feet or so of it below the neck, to very limited use. Mostly, it transported my head from dining tables to classes to bed, stopping to occasionally point it at the TV. It was a waste of a body, and my appearance — pudgy, pale, bepimpled — wouldn't have inspired anyone to disagree. My father was no Adonis — nobody in my lineage of stocky Jews has been, or will ever be, employed as an Abercrombie and Fitch model — but I could see the muscles in his legs, and he could walk up stairs without gasping, which seemed impressive enough. If he had looked like Arnold Schwarzenegger or Bruce Jenner — if he had those long, striated legs as on the cover of *The Complete Book of Running*

— I never would have attempted to emulate him. Instead, I would have just left to find my real parents.

This is what I remember about that first run: my orange Keds, slapping against the suburban asphalt for all of a half mile, and then my lungs exploding. I remember the gentle upward slope of a neighborhood street feeling like K2. I remember my father at my side, glancing at me occasionally, still not mocking, taking no vengeance, not then, not ever. I remember gasping that I was done, and then shuffling back home, wheezing and coughing, while he continued on methodically up the hill.

Many, many years later, I asked my father what he remembers about that day, and he said: "You came along in a pair of sneakers . . . and puffed as you ran. But you came the next morning, and then again. After a while, you asked for (and got) a pair of real running shoes. In a few months, you amused your adolescent self by running around me in circles."

He is correct. My improvement was so rapid — I was fifteen, for God's sake, which is a gift even to those otherwise ungifted — that one day soon after I started to run, on a beach in Florida, I literally ran in circles around my father while he ran straight up the beach, creating a pleasing helical pattern of footprints in the sand. I was laughing like a schoolboy, which I was, and running like an athlete, which I had never, ever dreamed of being. Within the year, I was traveling with my father to 10Ks and longer races around New Jersey. I'd start with him, then wait around the finishers' area for twenty minutes or more for him to methodically plod his way in, still looking like an idiot, but now no less, or more, than I did.

My running quickly went from casual to obsessive. I saw each community 10K as a new crucible to throw myself into in order to burn away some more of my excess. My times improved, edging downward asymptotically toward the forty-minute mark, but never quite beating it. I became good enough that I tried out for and was accepted onto my high school's mediocre cross-country team, coached by a teacher who knew less about running than I did, populated by kids who, unlike me, looked like runners. When I showed up the first day for practice, I was wearing a souvenir shirt from a 10K, and one of the other runners asked if I had actually run it, or, perhaps, scavenged it from a corpse. That day, I remember, I went for my first practice run with the team and waxed him. I don't know if I ever ran that well again.

My cross-country career lasted only a single season, and it wasn't particularly successful, partially because of a terrible bout of food poisoning and partially because as much as I loved to race, I hated to be beaten, which I was regularly, like a drum announcing the hour. So many people ran in the community 10Ks I favored that I never had a hope of winning, but I couldn't really lose, either, and instead ran for myself, to improve my own time. In a competitive cross-country race, a few won and many lost, and I always lost against all those taller, athletic kids with the natural ability and competitive instinct. All I had to offer was a kind of native stubbornness which faded the more I lost. I walked away from the team after my one year, deciding that the best roads to run on were the ones where my only competition was my past, slower self. As they say: Those who can't play sports, run. Those who can't run, run long.

Then came college, and very little time to run, and the discovery that — as with many other talents I thought I had — my running was much less impressive at Harvard than it had been in Berkeley Heights, New Jersey. Many of the other students zipping by me on the banks of the Charles River — when I could find a half hour to put on my old Pumas — were legitimate track and cross-country stars, who passed me as if the hedge funds they'd soon be managing were just across the next bridge. In my senior year, I had a brief but passionate romance with a young woman who had left her prior boy-friend for me; when she changed horses again, the next steed was a ROTC officer who ran the Boston Marathon our senior year. A marathon? It seemed crazy, or superhuman, or both. My girlfriend left me for an insane superhero, one who might tear the head off my body, if he could catch me. Which he could, easily.

And so it went, through my twenties and into my thirties. For five years right out of college, I lived in Los Angeles, where run-ning seemed dangerous enough to dissuade me. One night, I was running on the beach in Long Beach when suddenly I was blinded as a spotlight from the sky bathed me in a bright circle of white light. I looked up expecting an alien ship and instead saw a police helicopter; somebody was having some fun. Eventually, I realized all that brown stuff hanging around the horizon was being sucked into my lungs whenever I ran, and I gave up running to devote myself to more practical forms of exercise, like failure.

Then came a move across the country and a career and a wife and a job and kids and more and more moves, interspersed with the occasional spate of running, until a day in 2002 when I went in to the doctor for a routine physical. I stepped up on the scale, and the doctor flicked the sliding piece of pig iron with his finger.

"Height, five seven," he said. "Weight . . . uh . . . two hundred pounds."

He didn't hear my screaming. It must have been muffled by all that fat.

I began to jog again. I read *Absolutely American,* a terrific book about the military academy at West Point by David Lipsky, and became mildly obsessed with the story of one cadet, Jewish and stout, like me, who simply could not manage the running portion of the Academy's physical fitness requirement. He kept trying to run the army standard — two miles in seventeen minutes — and kept failing. Two miles in seventeen minutes: I had been able to do that, once. I put my middle daughter, aged two, into our running stroller and set out, instructing her to yell "Faster, Papa, faster!" It took me a few tries, and a few girlish yells, but I did it. So did the cadet, by the way, although he didn't have the use of a motivational toddler.

Then we moved into a new house, a big, old, four-story Victorian, and soon after that, I woke up one morning to see runners zipping by; as it happened, the course of my suburb's annual 10K went right by our front yard. A 10K? I used to do those. The next year, 2004, I entered the race. Did pretty well, too: around forty-five minutes. I was thirty-nine. I was four months from turning forty. I was afraid of dying. I decided to run the 2005 Chicago Marathon the next fall, on the theory that if I did that, I would not die. You may mock, but it has worked so far.

I made every rookie training mistake there was to make — I trained alone, I overdid it early, I injured myself, I aggravated the injury through more running, so I was forced to take a month off — and the marathon itself was incredibly painful. By the time I got to mile 22, a miserable desolate stretch of freeway access road north of Comiskey Park, I would have quit, happily, except if I ever wanted to finish a marathon, I'd have to run twenty-two miles all over again and that seemed far more painful that the measly four miles I had to limp through now. I stumbled through

Bronzeville and willed myself up Michigan Avenue, and then I climbed the overpass of Roosevelt Road like it was Everest and turned left and stumbled through the finish line and then, miserable and in pain and trembling from dehydration and exhaustion, I said to myself something I did not expect to hear myself say, something that became a hinge between my former life and my present, and led to, among many, many other things, the writing of this book.

"I wonder if I could do that faster."

Perhaps you would like to start running. You never have tried before, or you did and you hated it, and now you wonder how to begin moving in a way that will keep you going.

Get up. Start. Go. Move. Take a rusty first step, like the Tin Man. You will squeak. Go.

Do not buy anything first. Jim Fixx was right: you have everything you need right now. Someday you might buy better shoes, or specialized clothing, but you do not need them now. You do not need a gym membership or a treadmill or special shoes with rockers built into the soles. We have a tendency to purchase things with the expectation that they will improve us or cause us to become fitter, more active, but we believe this because we are the helpless objects of a multibillion-dollar, century-long campaign to convince us this is so, and partially because as a civilization we are only a few hundred years removed from believing that praying to the bones of saints would cure our arthritis. In fact, we are still in the thrall of superstition: there is little difference between a man in Detroit buying sneakers with Michael Jordan's image on them in the hope that it will help him jump farther and a Chinese man buying powdered rhino horn in the hope that it will make him more virile. No difference at all, in fact, other than the fact that the process is significantly less painful, and final, for Michael Jordan than it is for the rhino. It is all sympathetic magic: the atavistic human belief that we can impart to ourselves the essence of a thing via an image or symbol of that thing.

No: you have everything you need to begin. If you don't have sneakers, just grab your most comfortable shoes, or go barefoot on dirt or sand. If you don't have shorts, get an old pair of jeans and cut off the legs. If anybody judges you for wearing ratty clothes, one of the privileges and benefits of running is leaving people behind.

Every first step is the same, every last step is different.

You step outside, because real running is done outside, dammit, in the open air, where the endorphins hide. You hitch up your pants or adjust your sports bra and swing your arms a bit, and you imagine the next twenty minutes or two hours with excitement or apprehension or the kind of grim determination you might apply to eating something horrible in front of the person who made it, just to be polite.

You lift one leg and swing it out, and then spring the other leg, contracting the calf to flex the toes, and for one brief moment you fly upward, but you fail to fly and fall onto the extended heel of your forward foot, and you try to fly again and again and again and you fail and fail and fail and then you are down the street or road or driveway and the run has become what it will be, different from every other run you'll ever have or attempt, because every time you run you leave a little something on the road, and you pick up something to replace it. Every step and every run is a transformation from what you were into what you are becoming: a runner.

But that is not the same kind of transformation as what is promised by the fitness clubs or the weight loss ads or the Bowflex infomercials. Those promise all of us poor suckers who hate ourselves a chance to transform into something else, something bigger or smaller or glossier or younger, something that can be oiled and lit. The muscle and fitness magazines on the airport kiosks are parasites sucking on the fleshy folds of the self-loathing, and they belong not with the other athletic magazines but with the tattoo and fetishist magazines, because they are for people who recoil from what they see in the mirror and want to erase it.

Running isn't even like other sports. If you play tennis, you master movements and learn reflexes that are essentially unnatural; no Pleistocene man ever swung a racket, and this is even more true for stranger sports like football or lacrosse or water polo or whatever latest version of Centrifugal Bumble-Puppy the guys on ESPN16 are playing these days. When you run, you're actually trying to forget everything you've learned about moving, and trying to remember how to do something you've forgotten. Try it now; put the book or iPad down and run around the room. There, you did it, pick me up again.

Both Bruce Springsteen and Christopher McDougall say we are born to run, and who are we to argue? Running may be the answer to one of the oldest mysteries of evolutionary biology: How exactly did humans ever survive once we dropped (or were thrown, with some disgust) out of the trees? We have no claws, no terrible jaws, and we have a tenth of the strength of our nearest relative, the chimpanzee. We have our brains, but protohumans developed and thrived for a million years before the "great leap forward" of fifty thousand years ago, when a small band of *Homos* in Africa truly became *sapiens* and rapidly spread all over the world with their tools and culture to dominate the planet and eventually invent the Snuggie. No: we had some other secret weapon, beyond and before our ability to wonder what it might be. The best guess as to what it might have been lies in the answer to another evolutionary question, one that's apparent every time you look in a mirror: Why aren't you covered with fur, like every other living primate? What happened to our luxurious simian pelts? Darwin says it's because at some point in our distant ancestral past, it became more advantageous for our species to lose its fur than to keep it. But why? Almost every other land mammal sports thick fur or hair, testifying to its utility as insulator, camouflage, and protector of the fragile skin. Whatever we gave up fur for, it must have been important.

The secret to the survival of that bizarre hairless ape, precariously balanced on two legs, with its underbelly exposed to whatever efficient predator might want to casually disembowel it between bites of less stringy prey, is that it can run. We are evolved to run. Or we were "intelligently designed" to run, if you're stupid.

Our hairless bodies let us sweat and cool, our muscles can store enough energy for hours of effort, our lungs keep the fires burning. A cheetah can run at a speed of sixty miles per hour, but only in short bursts, after which it has to sit down and read a magazine. But we humans can just keep on going, the Energizer Bunnies of the Serengeti. Not fast, like a cheetah or an antelope, or even in impressive mass stampedes like buffalo or horses or Walmart shoppers. But slowly, methodically, rhythmically, and for a long time, with a persistence that was as deadly to our prey as it was annoying. "Why the hell won't that thing stop?" the exhausted emu said to itself, before lying down and just giving up, as we jogged up behind it, hungrier than we were before we started after it, or so argues McDougall, who describes the last living example of persistence hunters, a small tribe in Africa, in his book *Born to Run.* Bruce

Springsteen's explanation of why we run is to get the hell out of New Jersey.

And now, a million years later, as you get up every second day just to do another three miles around the housing development, heaving and breathing and trying to distract yourself with a new podcast, you are actually becoming, in tiny increments, the thing you were meant to be. The soft fat stored from a modern diet of processed industrial compounds starts to dissolve and drop away; your unused muscles in your legs start to tighten and firm; your lungs fill and empty and fill and become elastic and clear. Your heart, that small beating thing, strains to meet the stress and finds that it can. You can feel it growing in your chest cavity, like the Grinch's.

It's like one of those modern vampire or zombie movies, where some strange compound transforms the human body into something else, something much stronger, something much more dangerous than the weak and pasty suburbanites who become its prey. Instead of the Walking Dead, we are the Running Living. The urge to transform can come from within, from a sense of either loss or surfeit in your life. I have known people who ran because they felt there was something missing, and they thought if they could pick up some speed they might find it. I have also known people who've found themselves laden like Marley's ghost, with chains of stress and responsibility and unwanted pounds, who began to run in the hope that all or some of it would shake off from the jostling. Heraclitus said, "What does not change is the will to change," and thus our motivations are inexhaustible as we propel ourselves doggedly down the dawn streets. We are fueled by Gatorade and dissatisfaction.

One of my heroes is Dan Savage, the author, sex advice columnist, and activist. Dan and I have some significant things in common: we are the same age, we are obsessive exercisers because we are terrified of getting fat (though Dan favors the gym rather than the roads), and we both love musical theater. Of course, Dan is also (famously, proudly) gay, argumentative, incredibly profane, and knows more about something called "sounding" than I ever want to. In fact, I only know what sounding is because I read about it in one of Dan's columns, and I regret it to this day. I urge you not to look it up.

Dan is a prolific coiner of neologisms and aphorisms — his most famous being "It Gets Better," which is what he called the project in which he and his husband — as well as, eventually, thousands of other people, including the president of the United States — recorded messages for troubled or abused gay youth who needed hope for their future lives. He also came up with the "campsite rule" for relationships with much younger partners — leave them in better shape than how you found them — and the shorthanded advice DTMFA, or "Dump the motherfucker already," applied to cases in which a person is needlessly dithering over the latest in a long line of abuses and insults from their partner.

Also among Dan's coinages is GGG, for "Good, Giving, and Game," which are the qualities he says every person should strive to have as a sexual partner. To the extent it's not self-explanatory, I'll leave you to google "Dan Savage GGG" to let him explain it himself.

I came up with my own variation of GGG for new runners. In this case, it is: Gradual, Goal, and Group.

You need to make a gradual start because you're out of shape. What dissuades people from any new effort, at least most people, is the looming specter of failure. If you are unfit and you try to run a mile, you will collapse before it's over and agree to tell the

Nazis whatever they want to hear. Most people hate running not because there is something painful or inherently tortuous about running, but because it has been so long since the guileless runs of their childhood that they have lost all capacity for doing it. You'd hate eating, too, if you hadn't done it in thirty years and kept trying to put the food through the side of your cheek.

There's a saying in weight lifting: "train to failure," which means you want to stress the muscles to the point where they fail and you literally can't lift anymore. The notion is that the muscles will then repair themselves and grow bigger and stronger. Perhaps, but man, that hurts. I prefer another nostrum: don't practice failure, because then that's what you'll learn. If you try to learn to run by getting up and running till you exhaust yourself, you'll end up exhausted and frustrated. If you give yourself a goal that is tough enough to require effort but not so hard that you can't succeed, you can engineer success. The trick is to make it hard enough to give you a small but real benefit by doing it, which, by coincidence, is about the same level of intensity that maximizes self-satisfaction.

You are out of shape. You know you can't run a mile. But can you run, steadily, to the end of the block? Possibly. Maybe. You really don't know. You'll have to try it. You try it. You did it! Wow, that was tough, but you gutted it out until the Berkowitzes' driveway and from there to the end was pure Niestzschean will. Take a break, you deserve it. Walk a bit. Maybe to the end of the next block. And then, when you get there, run one more block.

You are basically treating yourself like a third grader at the start, giving yourself a participation medal for every day you get out of bed and get your shoes on. You are self-administering a dose of success, and you are trying to get yourself hooked. I am not talking about the legendary runner's high, the chemical effect of exercise-induced endorphins on the brain. I am talking about the pleasure of achieving something difficult — but not so difficult you can't achieve it.

Second: you want an achievable goal. As Paul Carrozza — the Austin, Texas, running guru who trained George W. Bush, Rick Perry, and a whole bunch of other people you have strong opinions about — said to me while we ran around Austin's Town Lake, "We don't help people exercise. Exercise is a chore. We train athletes. And training is a pleasure."

Let's say you would like to play guitar. (I

would.) It would be wonderful if you could simply play the songs you'd like to play, but instead you have to learn to play gradually: strings, notes, chords, practicing each step painfully until your fingers can learn the motions, and it becomes easy, and you can move on to the next step. You do this not because it is itself rewarding, but because you have a goal in mind: you want to play "Wrecking Ball" by Miley Cyrus, and you want to play it naked while wearing boots, like Miley Cyrus. This vision keeps you going, through the difficulty and the hesitation and the frustration. "Naked," you say to yourself, as your fingers ache to reach a barre chord. "Work boots," you think, as you realize you have no idea what a Gmaj7 chord even is, let alone how to play one. And so you persevere.

Now, imagine if you had to get up, every day, and do those same things, without any purpose but to train your fingers. The task set before you is to do nothing more than to play a scale and a series of chords in progressive order. You work your fingers for hours and hours until you can do something pointless. You wouldn't be enjoying yourself, you wouldn't be getting any better, and you certainly wouldn't be doing anything that could be called "playing the guitar." You'd be bored out of your mind, and you'd quit, as any sensible person would.

That's how most people approach running. They decide, for whatever reason, that they need to exercise, perhaps to lose weight, perhaps to "get in shape," though what shape, for what reason, is never specified. So they join a gym and get on the treadmill, or they buy one for their home, and then they do their thirty minutes or three miles, three times a week, defeating the screaming boredom by watching TV or listening to the radio and generally counting down the minutes until this chore is over.

Now this is better than nothing. Thirty minutes of aerobic activity three times a week is much better than indolence, and can in fact help you lose weight, regain muscle tone, improve your energy, and help win the war for the Allies, so if that's all you can do, and all you want to do, I say good for you and I have nothing more for you, except to comment that the only reason to watch *Morning Joe* at the gym on the 'mill is to be watching, live, on the day that Mika Brzezinski finally snaps and stabs Joe Scarborough to death with a mechanical pencil. Treadmills were invented as a form of forced labor in Victorian prisons — Oscar

Wilde was forced to work on one in Reading Gaol, powering a mill — and punishment for past sins, in my opinion, remains the only thing they're good for. Go outside.

But if you want to be a runner, find that goal. An excellent first one is a 5K, or a five-kilometer race. That translates to 3.1 miles and that is within the reach of just about everyone, barring disability or injury. They are common, with one or more happening just about every weekend in any metropolitan area, and they often are held to benefit worthy causes. There will be people at that race who intend to try to win it, and just might. But that won't be you. This will be unlike any other athletic contest you've ever tried, including intramural soccer and Ping-Pong tournaments, in that you will enter it with no notion of possibly winning. You will enter it to finish it, at a run.

The running press and the Internet are filled with programs such as Couch to 5K. None of them are objectively better than any other, although one might suit you and your schedule better, another worse. But each plan, if it's from a reputable source, will have the same general outline: gradual progression from no fitness to speak of (the notional "couch") to completing a 5K at a comfortable but still notable speed. Both the words "gradual" and "progression" are important. Any plan that starts you running too quickly or too far or for too long will burn you out within a week, and you'll recoil. But the plan has to increase the load on your muscles and heart so that you actually improve.

You will suffer, a bit. But as Paul Carrozza says, this time you are suffering for a concrete purpose — to arrive at the spring or fall or summer day when you will put on your shirt and shorts and tie your shoes and run a whole three miles without stopping. Instead of being Rocky Balboa going back and forth to his miserable job beating people up for a loan shark, you will be Rocky Balboa sprinting through the streets of Philadelphia on his way to his destiny. You will start when they fire a gun or sound a siren, you will run, you will finish when you step across a line and an announcer, with luck, says your name, rather than the name of the person right behind you or the one in right front of you. Then you'll get a medal, perhaps, and you will drink sports drink and eat a stale bagel that will be perfectly delicious and you will note your time — Thirty minutes? Maybe forty? — and you will say to yourself, perhaps: "Maybe I can do that faster."

The last "G" stands for "Group," and it's been the hardest of the three Gs for me to get people to accept. A lot of people say that they like running because it is a solitary sport, and it gives them a chance to be meditative and away from pressures and other people and blah blah blah; yes, I know, you value your alone time. But I think that for many people, including myself, we are reacting out of fear and discomfort. We don't want to go to classes because the perky trainer at the front makes us feel embarrassed, not to mention fat. We don't want to run in front of anyone; if we were good at sports, then we wouldn't be running, would we?

Get over it, and find a running group.

We humans, unless we are very strange humans, actually like other people; we enjoy talking to them, hanging out with them, and in some extreme cases, kissing them and making babies with them (which, not incidentally, provides more people to hang out with). Running with other humans is no different than any other pleasurable interaction, and in some ways it is much better, to wit: It is not an open-ended commitment. You are going for a run. It may last thirty minutes, it may last an hour or even two, but it will end. Even if the person you have chosen to run with was not a wise choice, you can rest easy in that the ordeal will be over relatively soon.

You do not have to worry about being sweaty, smelly, farting, burping, vomiting, or the occasional gastrointestinal distress. This is a run. Everybody is smelly, sweaty, farting, or something even more extreme. If you do not occasionally involuntarily expel something from your body while running, you're doing it wrong.

You do not have to worry about how you look. Running is the sport equivalent of a nudist camp. We simply accept each other as we are, for in any other direction lies madness.

You do not have to worry about being interesting. While running, anything becomes interesting, even the topic of running. Running is profoundly boring to talk about . . . except to other runners. Thus, don't think of your social runs as yet another time when you are obligated to be charming or fun or impressive — accept them as a time when you can be, and will be, gloriously dull. My running friends and I have had lengthy, interesting conversations about such topics as porta-potties, chafing nipples, and various kinds of shoelaces. We talk about stomach, muscular, and uterine cramps; we talk races and pacing and shoes; we talk about all the minutiae of running and no one leaves, because we're all constantly leaving together.

You don't even have to look anyone in the eye, if that causes stress. Everybody's looking ahead.

I should probably mention at this point that running sometimes sucks. There's no point in hiding it from you, and later on we'll speak more about it. There will be days on which the weather is awful, the footing terrible, the mood black, the stomach unhappy, the legs aching, and the head woozy. But misery, as is well known, loves company, and more to the point, like most burdens, sharing this one makes it lighter. Running thirteen miles in a rainstorm by yourself is miserable, stupid, pointless, and the sort of thing that will make you reconsider indolence, obesity, and an early death. The same experience with a band of friends is your very own St. Crispin's Day, a shared misery, a story you will tell and retell again and again until you get bored of it, which will be never.

Seven or eight years ago, my running friends and I went for a run on a sub-zero freezing day and decided, on the advice of one of them, to run a trail through a woods, including across a frozen snow-covered stream. My foot broke through the ice, and I soaked my running shoe and sock in the frigid water.

We've told the story of that day four hundred times since then, and it gets better every time. I believe in the latest iteration I was submerged into the ice up to my waist and I remained frozen there, like Satan in the lowest level of Dante's Inferno. If I had been alone, it would have been just a private misery, the memory of which would occasionally make me shudder for a few years after. Because I was with a group, it's a glorious story of adversity defeated. Then again, if I had been alone, I wouldn't have run into the goddamn stream.

And, insofar as we are naturally social animals, we are also naturally competitive. I don't mean we wish to triumph over our friends, although that can be a fun way to spend an afternoon if you've got time to kill and a set of Settlers of Catan. What I mean is that we tend to measure ourselves against other people, because measuring ourselves against other species or inanimate objects makes no sense. We will never be as adorable as that puppy, or as tall as that cell phone tower. But we might, if we try, be as fast as our friend Ken, who is roughly our age, height, and weight. We might even beat him someday.

Your running friends should be roughly at your level of fitness, with similar goals. You get no benefit from running with people you can't keep up with, or who can't keep up with you. But the key word is "roughly" — ideally, you should be the second-slowest person in your group. Having a number of friends who are constantly just ahead of you at the track, just a little more comfortable and faster in the long runs, who can go just a little farther without a break, means you will be constantly pushing yourself to catch up, keep up, and keep going, and pressing your limits means you will be constantly improving. Any running is good; but running just on the edge of your ability, after comfort and before crisis, is the best. You will come to love your running friends, and you will express your affection for them by trying to kick their asses, or at least keeping them from kicking yours.

Why the second slowest? Because it sucks to be last.

Finally, of all the people we know, we are often the least kind to ourselves. We are the ones we disappoint, we are the ones we mistreat, we are the ones we betray by going back on promises to improve and to

Never Make That Mistake Again. We are the ones we punish most. If you say to yourself, I am going to get up and run every other day because it's Good For Me, then "Me" is going to be going without that run within a few weeks. But if you have agreed to be on the corner of Sixth and Main at 6 AM to meet the guys for your run, then before you turn over and go back to sleep you will have to grapple with the fact you are going to be Letting Those Guys Down. What you would do to yourself without a care of the cost, you'll hesitate about doing to the guys. So you'll get up and you will go. And there you will find the guys, who have shown up, despite the early hour, despite the darkness and the fatigue, because they didn't want to let you down. They're better to you than you are.

It's also possible that running friends might become your friends in real life. This can be odd, because it's strange to see people you normally see sweaty and in short pants dry and in trousers, and so I don't recommend it, but hey, it's your life. Do what you want.

But find a group. What is coming your way will be more easily handled with a show of force.

THREE

It was two o'clock in the afternoon and 30 degrees out — warm for a day in mid-February, which was fortunate because I was standing on Market Street in St. Louis in my underwear, next to a guy dressed as Braveheart, without a shirt but with face paint (blue) and a sword (foam). I waved my arms around, trying to stay warm without hitting anybody with the Cupid's bow and arrow I was holding. Then the starter, such as she was, cupped her hands around her mouth and yelled "Go!" and everybody started running, except for me, because Braveheart decided to rally the three hundred nearly naked people behind us by swinging his sword, which whacked me hard in the face. He took off. I grabbed at my nose, swore, hitched up my red boxer briefs, and chased after him.

Welcome to the beta test of life as a divorced dad.

This was an intentional test run. It was the winter of 2013, about two months before the Boston Marathon, a race that, on this cold day, I had no notion I would be running. My wife and I had agreed, in January, to separate and then divorce, and my soon-to-be ex had taken the kids to visit her parents in Minnesota. Under the circumstances, she suggested, it might be awkward for me to accompany them. Perhaps I should have argued, but they had taken such trips without me before, and this seemed like a strange time to insist on coming along. Besides, there was no time like the present to start getting used to the future as a part-time parent.

At the same time, I didn't want to mark this first Solo Divorced Dad Weekend by lying around the house eating takeout in my underwear and watching porn. That seemed to be a bad way to set the tone. Instead, I would do a road trip of my own. How about St. Louis? I had friends there, and it was also about a day's drive away, and happily, psychologically, and geographically in the opposite direction. But I needed a better excuse. One of the habits I have been criticized for in the bosom of my family — justly — is constantly needing some sort of activity to amuse myself, rather than just, you know . . . being. So what could I do? A race? I liked to do races. One of my St. Louis friends told me about a race a friend of hers was doing. Something called the Fourth Annual Cupid's Undie Run. Whatever. I'm in.

On New Year's Eve 2009, a twentysomething in Washington, DC, named Bobby Gill was talking with his friends Chad Leathers and Brendan Hanrahan (who were also, I am sure, in their twenties) about doing something for Chad's younger brother, who was afflicted with neurofibromatosis, or NF, an extremely unpleasant pediatric disease that causes chronic tumor growth. All three friends were runners, so they thought of a fund-raising race, but then said to one another, "Why do another 5K? Nobody remembers a 5K!" and came upon the idea of running in their underwear. (This is how I know they were in their twenties: they just assumed that their friends wouldn't mind running in public in their underwear.) They decided they needed a holiday to link it to for marketing purposes, one that was coming up soon. . . . Martin Luther King Jr. Day? Not quite right. Valentine's Day! Great. Then it will be red underwear.

I called Bobby on my way down to St.

Louis, and he told me they'd expected about fifty of their friends to show up that first time and strip to their skivvies before doing a guerrilla sprint on the sidewalks circling the Capitol, but word spread around the DC running community with the speed of a nearly naked young person trying to get out of the cold. On February 13, 2010, more than six hundred people swarmed Capitol Hill, a mass of jiggling, goose-pimpled bare flesh, raising $10,000 for the Children's Tumor Foundation. Three Valentine's Days later, in February 2013, the race was held in fourteen US cities, plus Sydney, Australia, with thousands of participants attempting to reach a $1 million goal.

For me, there would be two very unusual things about the race, and that did not include the underwear. First, perhaps because of the cold weather, perhaps because they wanted to attract a wider pool of participants than the cadre of hard-core runners, Bobby and co had set the distance at one mile. And further, it would be informal, untimed, and not even accurately measured. Call it a "mile-ish." You know, out thataway for about a half mile or so, then turn back. I made a note to myself: don't try to set an international record for the mile distance, because it won't count.

Second, it was for charity. This may seem like a bonus, but for a "serious runner," charity running can have a disreputable air. The Boston Marathon, as said, requires entrants to qualify by running a sufficiently fast time at a prior accredited marathon. To run Boston, you have to earn it. Or, if you don't want to put in the work, sign up with some charity, promise to raise (or donate) a set amount of money, and they'll give you a bib. Easy. Then there are the countless charitable organizations that promise to help you train up to run a marathon or half marathon, all for a large fee that mostly, probably, goes to the charity, rather than the coaches and T-shirts and other accoutrements of Very Public Do-Gooding. This sort of stuff made me narrow my eyes and sniff and think that if you really wanted to train for a marathon, you should grind out the miles in misery, unsupported, like God intended.

But I needed some distraction on my first Divorced Weekend. Having run countless half marathons and 10Ks and ten-milers, a "mile-ish" run in my underwear on a cold winter day seemed like it would be, at least, a significant change of pace.

But if I was going to raise money, even on a lark, then dammit, I would raise some money. I only had a week to fund-raise after deciding to run the race, but I went to it with a vengeance: I set up a donation page and then tweeted out appeals, offering to post a picture of myself running in my underwear when I met my $1,000 goal, and then, when that goal was quickly reached, I announced that if I hit $2,000, I wouldn't post it.

Over the course of my single week of fund-raising, I began tracking the thermometer-style money graph on my fund-raising site like it was an indicator of my value as a human being. In response to many lewd suggestions as to what under-wear I should wear, I posted an offer: anybody who donated $500 could dictate my costume. I was amazed, and more than a little worried, when somebody took me up on it. But I put my qualms aside. I was raising money! Lots of it! Anything to make that needle move — and it was moving. As far as addictions involving needles went, I could do worse.

Still, I was nervous when I walked into Syberg's bar in St. Louis on the Saturday of the race, and not just because of what I was wearing (and not wearing) under my sweats. The place was packed with people, mostly young, mostly drinking, and mostly naked.

Very few of them — by my informal survey, which I conducted by asking them — had ever run a race before. Most of them had no knowledge or interest in NF or the Children's Tumor Foundation but had shown up, it seemed, because drinking beer and gallivanting around in their underwear in public on a Saturday afternoon "sounded like fun." So, as it turns out, there are hobbies stranger than running.

There were some older folk mixed into the crowd, and although they seemed to be grinning as much as anyone else, they were there for a more serious purpose. Every person I spoke to over the age of thirty-five, including Amanda, the race director, was there because of a direct connection to a child suffering from NF. A group of older runners had brought one such child, the daughter of one of their coworkers. Lexi seemed shy and frail but delighted to be surrounded by so much determined love. One of Lexi's supporters told me their employer, the St. Louis area water utility, was suspicious and worried about this "undie" thing and insisted they run clothed, which is why the entire group was wearing extra-large unmentionables over tights and T-shirts. She seemed regretful.

And me? Having stripped off my sweats, I

was talking to this perfectly nice complete stranger in the outfit decreed by my $500 donor: a pair of red boxer briefs with the words KNICKERS OF GLORY written on the butt, red feathered wings on my back, a Cupid's bow and arrow in my hands, and a heart shaved into my chest hair. I envied the utility worker in her tights. At that point, I would have preferred a burka.

I ordered a beer from the bar. I would have had another, but naked and shivering and shaved and drunk seemed one adjective too far. So I shuffled outside and waited with the crowd, most of them much younger and much more attractive than me, although few of them were more naked. The race started. I got hit in the face with a foam sword. Then I whooped and ran.

At first I gave in to my usual instinct and tried to keep up with the leaders, a few skinny guys who hadn't laden themselves with props. But after about a hundred yards I actually said out loud, "What am I doing?" and slowed down, circled back, and joined the vast unclothed masses. This was supposed to be fun. And today, there was no fun in me being out in front . . . especially for the people right behind me.

The turnaround point was a half mile up a slight hill, and before we were very far up it, a lot of the cuties in their undies were walking, either due to too little training or too much alcohol. They were all still laughing, and so was I. I had never been in an event like this; hardly dressed, hardly running, in what was hardly a race. Then I decided I wanted to get to the finish line to watch people as they came in, so I sprinted the last few hundred yards. Somebody shouted out, "Not fair! He's got wings!" I jumped to make them flap.

At the finish, people laughed and hollered and cheered as they completed their mile run as if they had just won the Olympic marathon. They hugged their friends, an act more sweaty and intimate than usual, and everybody immediately retired into the bar for more beer. There, the organizers quieted the DJ and took over the bar's PA system. They announced best costume — some twenty-year-old in something revealing — and then they announced the event's big winner, the top individual fund-raiser.

It was me.

My wheedling, my begging, my bargaining, my offers to wear whatever ridiculous thing my big donors suggested, had brought in $4,000 for the Children's Tumor Foundation, and I accepted my medal (in the shape of underwear, of course) with a huge grin.

It was the first time I'd ever won a race of any kind, by any measure. And it struck me, as I grinned and grinned, standing in my underwear in front of a crowd, that I had picked a great one to win. I have run thousands of miles for myself, and one, just one lousy mile up a hill and back, for some sick kids I had never met, and at that moment, it seemed to me the only mile I'd ever run that mattered.

Clutching my medal, my costume safely and securely concealed again under my sweats, I walked back to my hotel and wondered if that was true. Had all the miles I'd run, all the races I'd finished, all the PRs I'd set, been useless, other than this silly informal jog up and down a cold St. Louis boulevard? Obviously not — I had lost weight, gained energy, learned discipline and focus, generally improved my health and disposition — but what good did any of it do? What is running for?

Once upon a time, of course, it was essential. Even after we left the hunter-gatherer stage, the ability to move quickly over ground proved essential to all kinds of human pursuits, most importantly the violent ones. A horse, obviously, can outrun a human, but a human can run longer without tiring, even beating the horse in a marathon, at least on a hot day. (Horses overheat; we sweat.) According to legend, when the Greeks needed to send word of their victory at Marathon back to Athens, they didn't send a horseman or a pigeon — they sent a man, Phidippides, who ran the whole way, delivered the message, and died — the worst postrun celebration ever. Even in World War II, messages were sent across a battlefield by use of "runners," who, we can presume, ran.

But now . . . well, sometimes you get to the bus stop just as the bus is leaving, and if you run you might be able to get up to the door and get the attention of the driver, and if she's in a generous mood she might stop the bus and let you on. But otherwise, running, as a skill, seems to have no practical value in this world.

This used to bother me a lot back in high school, when the various things I could do — write, act, make smart-ass remarks — didn't do much to impress anyone (by which I mean girls) and the things I couldn't do — play sports, purchase beer, have clear skin — seemed unobtainable. So over the course of many, many solitary laps run around my suburb, I came up with a scenario that went something like this:

FADE IN

DEEP WOODS — DAYTIME

A LOVELY YOUNG WOMAN lies on the ground, a snakebite on her thigh. A DOCTOR cradles her head as she bravely fights for life.

DOCTOR

She only has two hours to live, and the only antidote is five miles away! We have no transportation and no way to communicate! She's doomed unless . . . someone here can run ten miles in ninety minutes or less!

THE FOOTBALL STAR, THE CLASS PRESIDENT, and THE HANDSOME MUSICIAN look down helplessly.

PETER steps forward. He peels off his jacket, revealing a running singlet.

PETER

I'll be right back.

In the course of my marriage, I would often compare my sole hobby, even as I began to get good at it, to my wife's. Raised by crafty Midwesterners, she could cook, sew, draw, play the piano, sing, and decorate a house. Me, I could run. Maybe after an apocalypse, I could fetch far-off supplies. Couldn't be something heavy, though, because it's hard to run while carrying things. Your hand gets sweaty if you hold it, and a backpack bounces around.

Of course, something happens every day in every country around the world in which the ability to run far and relatively fast is essential to success. I was just blind to it, because I'm an American.

I am utterly oblivious to the charms of soccer 99 percent of the time, but then every four years, during the World Cup, I fall in love for the first time again, an Eternal Sunshine of the Footieless Mind. A few years ago, I was watching the games, marveling anew at the players' grace and athleticism — I'm an oaf — their astonishing skills — I can hardly kick a can — and their running . . . wait a minute.

Soccer has to be the most running-intensive sport there is; the widely accepted estimate is that elite midfielders run a full ten kilometers, or about six miles, during a match. So, one day in front of the TV, I asked myself: could a middle-aged man, with no skills, no experience, and no real understanding of the game, but with a bouquet of marathon finishers' medals, hold his own on a soccer field?

Or to put it another way — could my ability to run a few miles without vomiting actually, finally, have some positive use?

I put out a tweet; it was answered by Emily White, a Chicago-area singer-songwriter and longtime soccer enthusiast, and a few emails later I was a proud member of Team Orange in the Chicago Metropolitan Sports Association, an LGBT recreational sports league. Jonathan, the league organizer, said, "If you have never played before and have no knowledge of the game, then you will fit right in on that team."

First lesson: Soccer players can be catty. At least, these soccer players.

I bought myself some shin guards for twelve dollars but figured old running shoes would suffice instead of cleats, especially since I had no idea if I would last past the first five minutes of the game. (My one prior attempt at soccer, at an intradorm match in college, had lasted exactly three minutes, until I stood wondering how I might get the ball away from an opponent, and he ran straight into me, knocking me out cold.) On a Saturday morning by Lake Michigan, I put on my new Team Orange jersey, shook hands with my new teammates (including the catty Jonathan), carefully and repeatedly warned them of my utter ignorance, and took to the field — rather, the pitch. See? Learning already.

I was assigned to defense, which I assumed was the soccer equivalent of right field, where I spent most of my Little League baseball career. I was joined there by a pink-shirted opponent named Sean, whom I was supposed to defend. Sean was about six inches taller than I was, at least ten years younger, and chances were good he had played this game before. But I figured if he was posted out here with me, he must suck too, and how many marathons had he run, huh? I wondered if there would be a chance, given the rules of the game, to actually run circles around him.

The game began. It didn't have the lightning pace or surgical passes of World Cup action, so as the first few minutes went by I found myself standing around and idly watching the muddled action in the distance — again, much like Little League. But then a Pink player kicked the ball downfield to Sean, who received it with a distressing amount of skill and took off down the field toward our goal. I gave chase.

And I couldn't catch him.

This was alarming. I honestly thought that I would be the best runner on either team — did I mention my eleven marathons? — but this wasn't loping a long distance, this was mad sprinting, fifty feet at a time, and as much as I leaned forward and dug those old shoes into the turf, I couldn't outrun him. Another defender intercepted Sean, kicked the ball clear, and the action moved back to midfield. I gave Sean another look and realized — finally — that even if poorer players were relegated to defense, as I had been, he played for the other team. He was a forward — an attacker. The prestigious position, reserved for the most skilled, and, as I had just found out, the fastest players. This didn't look good.

Orange and Pink were evenly matched, and the action flowed back and forth. Pink was more aggressive and had some skilled midfielders, so the ball was often down at our end. The action for me was moments of repose interposed with more mad sprinting. I kicked the ball once or twice — in the right direction — and even managed a header. I eventually began to think tactically . . . depending on where the ball was, I could move forward a fair distance toward the Pink goal, relying on my one skill to get me back in time if the action were reversed.

Sean's skills completely overwhelmed me, as you'd expect; I never once managed to get the ball away from him. But, as I eventually realized, I didn't have to, and I didn't have to overtake him. If I could just keep pace with him as he ran down the field, keeping myself between him and the Orange goal, he couldn't take a good shot — he had to either pass (and a better Orange defender would intercept) or try a weak shot right into our excellent goalie's arms. I like to think that he started to get frustrated — who was this short bald guy who could hardly get a foot on the ball, but who just wouldn't get the hell out of the way?

The whistle blew at fifty minutes, with a score of 0–0. I never got to show everybody the Goal Celebration I had planned, which involved a backflip and some Western line dancing. But Team Pink didn't get to do any celebrations either. Because, in some tiny part, they couldn't get past me.

My GPS watch, which I kept running between whistles, showed an elapsed three miles run, which seemed a fair distance on a fifty-meter field. Most of that running was gentle jogging up and down the pitch, either following or anticipating the action, but there was a fair bit of mad dashing, usually in pursuit of Sean. I was tired, but not winded. I felt, appropriately enough, as if I had just run a fast 5K. To a great extent, my theory had proven true — at least in a recreational-level game, and at least on defense (i.e., not having to actually kick the ball toward a target), simply being able to run was a workable substitute for soccer competence.

My new teammates congratulated me on a good showing in my first soccer game ever.

"I like your hustle!" shouted our goalie.

I thanked him, sincerely, and said, "Hustle is all I got."

I meant to keep up my soccer career, but of course I did not. My life is too complicated, and my travel too constant, to join a team and actually show up on a regular basis. And the last thing I needed was another group of people for me to disappoint.

Back home from St. Louis, I rejoined my wife and daughters who had returned from Minnesota. As we waited for the Chicago weather to start to warm, the increasing tension in my house ground me down. One morning soon after the Cupid's Undie Run,

I got up in the dark from the attic room I had moved into, dressed as quietly as I could in a technical shirt, tights, a hat, and gloves, and sneaked down the stairway, doing my best to step on the front of the stair risers so as not to make a noise. There was enough disruption in the house without waking anybody up.

I jogged down the street to meet my running group. I could see them ahead of me, jumping up and down to keep warm while wearing their safety LED lights; they looked like a cloud of fireflies. And I would join them, and we would flit around the town, and return to the homes where we had started, having gotten nowhere, and learned nothing.

By this time, the glow from my fundraising win had long ago worn off, and I was dealing with familial and emotional issues that I had no clue how to handle, none of which were made any easier by cardiovascular fitness. As we started off that morning, I was gripped by the realization that all these years I had been training for the wrong challenge. Maybe the time and effort I had put into running would have been better spent learning to be a better parent, or husband, or — given the increasing level of tension between myself and my wife, and the seemingly unstoppable descent into open conflict — a more effective combatant. As it was, I felt useless, as if I had been practicing horsemanship for a decade and was now going into battle against tanks. Tanks with lasers.

But then I was struck with a sudden memory: It was three years earlier, and I was with my middle daughter, the same one who was now urging me to move out of the house so that everybody would stop being so mad. I was walking her and her younger sister to school, down the block, as I did most mornings, and we were late, as we were most mornings. Ahead of us, across the blacktop and playground, we could see the last straggling students entering the school, and the teacher's aide about to close the doors. We would be locked outside, forced to go around to the office to get (another) set of late passes, unless . . .

"Papa! Use your running powers!" she shouted.

I crouched, I smiled, and then I flew.

FOUR

As the weekend of the 2013 Boston Marathon approached, I found myself more and more grateful that I had agreed to run it. My domestic situation had deteriorated even further, and my home had turned into an unwilling host that was trying to eject me as if I were an infectious cell. I was less spoken to than spoken at. My absence was wished for so often and so vividly by my wife that the relief of giving in and leaving was greater than the satisfaction of defying her and staying. And by accepting an additional invitation, I got to leave a day early. Good job, me.

The marathon was held on a Monday, as it always is — Patriots' Day, the third Monday in April — but I headed to the airport on Saturday morning. My first stop was Hamilton, New York, where I was to give a presentation about the Constitution, based on the PBS special *Constitution USA with Peter Sagal* that was to be broadcast just a month later. In Hamilton, on the afternoon before my speech, I had been asked by a local running group to host a 5K race, starting from the town common, and as I looked around the group of runners, mostly college students, with mostly nifty expensive new shorts and singlets, most of them were adjusting headphones and picking out playlists before slipping their phones into their Velcro arm holsters. Most runners these days look like telephone operators in the 1950s: their ears are stuffed with other people's conversations.

I welcomed everybody to the race, made my usual jokes, made some stirring remarks about the running community, and then I started a sentence that I didn't exactly know how I was going to end. "Hey," I said. "I see a lot of you wearing headphones. And I'm going to make a suggestion: take them out."

They stared at me like I was a lunatic.

In my long years of running long distances, I also have made great use of headphones and iPods. For races, I used to program special race-day playlists, which would always begin with Bruce Springsteen's "Born to Run" (a cliché, I know) and end with OK Go's "Invincible," which

I loved not only for its anthemic encouragement — "When they finally come to destroy the earth/They'll have to go through you first" — but also because of Damian Kulash's sly aside, "When they finally come, what'll you do to them/Gonna decimate them like you did to me?" Nothing inspires last-minute effort more than bitter irony.

But after a while, I started to leave the headphones behind. First I gave them up for races. It occurred to me that if I was going to train and practice and focus on achieving something, when the time came to actually do it I could at the very least pay attention. A race, most especially and counterintuitively a marathon, requires more focus on the moment than someone who's never done it might imagine. We scan our bodies for discomfort, we check our pace, we count the miles and measure our remaining strength against the remaining distance. Besides, if you think of the great images of athletic achievement — Roger Bannister breaking the tape for the first four-minute mile, Dick Fosbury winning gold with his newfangled Fosbury Flop at the 1968 Olympics in Mexico City, Bobby Orr diving through the air as he won the Stanley Cup in 1970, catcher Jason Varitek picking up pitcher Keith Foulke after the Red Sox recorded the final out of the 2004 World Series — none of those people are, at that moment, listening to Squeeze's *Greatest Hits.*

Then as time went on, I started to give up my headphones for training runs as well. I am typing this, obviously, staring at a screen. The computer is also playing music, which I enjoy as I write. When I finish writing in a little bit, I will go have myself some lunch, and of course I'll play some music or news, and maybe even look at another screen. After lunch, I'll go rake some leaves or do other tasks, with headphones firmly in my ears; I'll enjoy music over dinner, and then finish my day by watching another, larger screen, with some content that, I hope, can command my entire attention.

If I don't leave my headphones behind when I run, I wouldn't spend a single minute of my waking life free from input.

I have a friend who wears headphones on long solo runs because, he says, "I can't spend that much time alone in my head." I disagree. He can, and he should. Spending that much time inside one's head, along with the voices and the bats hanging from the various dendrites and neurons, is one of the best things about running, or at least one of the most therapeutic. Your brain is like a duvet cover: every once in a while, it needs to be aired out.

I am conflict-averse by disposition and funny by profession, and like the unpopular flavors of soda pop, my darker, angrier, and more earnest thoughts tend to accumulate in the dispenser and gum up the works. When I decide to run alone, with nothing in my ears but the air and the occasional gnat, it gives me a chance to rehearse the things I'm too shy or self-conscious to actually say, and to put them into words with the help of my constant left-right-left metronome.

Often, my inner monologues are serious responses to the daily news my day job forces me to joke about — speeches that might be delivered from presidential podiums or witness stands or news desks that the actual person in question just apparently isn't smart enough to give. They should consult me — in my inner cable news channel, my speechwriting always works, and almost always inspires a standing ovation, groveling apology, or both.

Sometimes, of course, these perorations are quite personal. In the declining years of my marriage, as our fights became more constant, and more frustrating, my runs became the place where I could say the things I was either too weak or wisely cautious to say out loud, condemnations and defenses that were never contradicted or interrupted because I was saying them into the air. On my runs, unlike in real life, there are no rebuttals, no counterarguments, no ripostes beginning with "Well, how about the time *you* —" In my running mind, and only there, my opponents are dumb with sheepish recognition.

And every time I let off this toxic steam — rising and evaporating with the other noxious gases from my sweaty self — I can feel the tension leave my arms and legs, and my gait becomes looser and freer. I come from a long line of shoulder-hunchers, and as I rant and I run I can feel my back straighten and my head rise. It's as if the dark thoughts I give silent voice to are quite literally holding me down, weights tied to my neck and clavicles, and as I indulge them I cut them and let myself rise again.

And then, as my vents clear, I begin to think about running. Our sport seems mindless only to people who never run long enough for any thought to form other than "When can I stop running?" But the only way to succeed as a long-distance runner is to do it mindfully, to be aware of the body and the world it is moving through.

I think about my motion, and my breathing, my muscles, and their state of agitation or stress or relaxation. I note my surroundings — the downward slope I would never notice driving this street, the hawk's nest I would never see for lack of looking up, the figure in a window caught in a solitary moment of their own. I think about the true meaning of distance — about the learning that comes from running a mile in your own shoes. I think about blisters and bliss, and the voices quiet.

So, in Hamilton, New York, on that April day, two days before the 2013 Boston Marathon, I looked out at the crowd and said, "Take off your headphones. A 5K is a little over three miles, and let's say you run a ten-minute mile, so that's about half an hour. You can spend half an hour without distractions. Pay attention to what you're doing, pay attention to your body, pay attention to your breathing. Some of you are about to run your first race ever — be here for it."

Some of the runners took my advice, taking off their headphones and stowing them in their bags. I watched those people as we all shuffled to the line, and started to watch for the first indication of someone spelunking into the darkest depths of their own head, their lips starting to move as their own inner monologues emerged to fill the sudden silence.

That evening was one of the first times I had lectured on the Constitution, and I decided to tell a slightly different story than the one related in the PBS documentary that would be premiering at a Washington event the next week, two days after the Boston Marathon. Instead of the issues addressed in the documentary — Federalism, the Fourteenth Amendment, the Commerce Clause, etc. — I wanted to address a basic question: why did our constitution work (with many exceptions for many people over the years) when so many other national constitutions have failed?

The question had rattled around in my own mind since I'd shared a casual conversation with Yale professor Akhil Reed Amar, the featured expert in our documentary. He had said, "You know, the Soviet Union had a bill of rights, too." A Google search showed me that it had. It's a really good one, in fact. It guaranteed all citizens liberty and equal rights, as well as housing, a decent income, and even vacations for all. Man, that sounded like a great place!

Obviously, the Soviet bill of rights was a

meaningless joke. The more important and more difficult question was why ours wasn't a joke. Our film crew did "man-on-the-street" interviews all over the country, from the line of customers waiting to buy medicinal marijuana in Oakland to a Tea Party Express rally in Appleton, Wisconsin, and our conclusion was: nobody knows anything about the Constitution of the United States. "What does the Constitution mean to you?" I would ask various people, and they would say, "Freedom!" (a word that does not appear in the main text of the Constitution) and if I were to ask, "Freedom to do what?" they would respond, "Whatever I want! That's America!" Sometimes they would argue that it gave them the right to carry guns wherever and whenever they liked, or to walk around naked if they wanted to do that, or to walk around naked with guns. Certainly, whatever the Constitution means, the people you don't like are obviously and clearly violating its spirit and have to be stopped.

A lot of people we met, like Steve DeAngelo, the cannabis activist who ran the clinic in Oakland, believe the Constitution affords states (like California) the right to do whatever they please (like legalize cannabis). Others, like Kris Perry and Sandy Stier, from geographically and philosophically nearby Berkeley, believe the Constitution prevents states (like California) from doing what the population of the state wants it to do, like banning marriages between same-sex partners, as California did in the state election of 2008. (Kris and her partner, Sandy, were co-plaintiffs, along with Paul Katami and Jeff Zarrillo, in the successful federal lawsuit against Proposition 8.) There are people like Gary Marbut, a gun rights activist in Montana who believes the federal government violates the Constitution by not protecting his right to sell his firearms to anyone he likes whenever he likes, and there are other people like Minnijean Brown Trickey, one of the Little Rock Nine, who feels the federal government violated the Constitution by not protecting her civil right to attend a desegregated high school, even though it once sent in the 101st Airborne Division to do just that.

So given all this sometimes vitriolic disagreement as to what the document means, I asked the audience in Hamilton: why does the Constitution continue to function? Because even if the citizens of this country don't know much about the Constitution — its language, its history, the complexities of constitutional law as established by two centuries of Supreme Court jurisprudence — they believe in it. Almost everyone in America, from peon to president, believes that we are ruled by laws, that everyone must subject themselves to a duly constituted government, and that we will settle disputes by peaceful (if sometimes rhetorically vicious) means. We all believe the solution to an election that doesn't go your way is the next election, not violent rebellion. We believe that the way to solve even the most bitter dispute with a neighbor is through the courts, not by firebombing their house.

If the principles of the Constitution are violated, the document itself does not flap its parchment wings and fly out of the National Archives to beat the reprobate about the head and shoulders until he relents and confesses his error. He is restrained, if he can be restrained, by a collective belief, a civic religion, an irrational faith in the power of democratic rule. Nixon, I pointed out, knew that if he handed over the Watergate tapes after the Supreme Court ruled against him in 1974, his presidency would be over. But if he didn't do what the court ordered, if he simply refused, what would have occurred? He was the one who had the army. But even Nixon knew what he had to do when the final choice had to be made. He knew that to do otherwise would instantly change his place in history from disgraced president to quite possibly the last president, the man who ended the American experiment.

Thus, I said to the happy people of Hamilton, the Constitution was and remains a communal agreement, an imaginary construct given weight and meaning by collective belief. It is the Tinkerbell of national charters — it only stays alive by our constant and enthusiastic clapping. If enough of us stop believing in it, if we reach some tipping point, unknowable until we reach it, when enough people cease to honor it or any of its provisions, then it will fade away, like the picture of Marty McFly and his siblings in *Back to the Future.*

Everybody laughed and clapped and nodded.

I've given that lecture many times since then, and it has occurred to me that there are a lot of other things that we take for granted as reality, as agreements and understandings that can't be broken. And then they are, and we are left gaping at the new paradigm like someone returning home to a house consumed by fire. How can something disappear so quickly and so completely? A home, a marriage, a family? "How could . . . ? What has . . . ? It was just here."

We live in a world of mutually assured hallucination. That which we imagine to be immutable is not. Those which we think of as laws are, to paraphrase *Pirates of the Caribbean,* merely suggestions. And if enough people decide to believe something else . . . then that other reality supplants our own. There were times, many of them, during the course of my first divorced year, when I would say to myself, "Things will have to get back to normal," not realizing that reality is democratically determined, and I only have one vote. Three years later, in 2016, this principle would be proved on a national level, although that too was something I then didn't have the capacity to imagine.

People enjoyed my presentation. I was taken out for a drink by my host, then I went to bed in my hotel, and in the morning I got up and flew to Newark to connect to Boston. Sitting in the Newark airport, waiting for my connecting flight, I realized that it had been (as far as I could remember) exactly forty years since my first airplane flight, when as a young Master Sagal of eight years, I had flown the same route, from Newark to Boston, to visit my grandmother. I remembered getting a cool metal pilot wings pin to put on my blazer, which I wore over my turtleneck sweater. As I got on the airplane, which I hoped was a different one than I had ridden forty years before, I told the flight attendant the story, and I asked her if they still had wings for traveling minors. She laughed and nodded and handed over what passes for souvenir airline pilot wings these days, a cheap-ass bit of plastic. Things really did seem to be on a downward slope. I pinned it to my shirt nonetheless, posted a selfie to Twitter, and settled in for the flight to Boston and the marathon.

I was nervous. Marathons are hard and I hadn't been adequately training for this one. A man named William Greer, whom I had never met, was going to be depending on me and he might prove to be foolish to have done so. I honestly didn't know what would happen.

It was the loudest noise I have ever heard. An enormous, percussive, deeply metallic
BANG
and it was close, close enough to feel as well as hear — about a hundred yards away, judging from the rising plume of smoke. Our view of the spot was blocked by the

superstructure of the finish line, the camera towers, and the armature of ceremony. We couldn't see what was happening.

Then there was a second
BANG
farther away. Another plume of smoke.

I like to believe, now, that at that moment, in that place, as the smoke dissipated into the sky, I considered walking toward the source of the sound to see what had happened. I am a curious human being and though not a journalist, I work for a prestigious journalistic organization and a very unusual and alarming thing had happened. A braver man might have at least tried to get a closer look.

Instead I just stood there, and a woman said to me, "What do you think it was?"

And I said, "I don't know, maybe a power transformer?"

The woman: "Maybe a car backfired."

"Too loud for that."

"You think it's a bomb?"

"No way," I said. "I mean, seriously? A bomb?"

I met that woman again, two years later, at a function for Team With A Vision. She introduced herself to me as "the woman who was standing next to you when the bomb went off." I quizzed her carefully as to how far away she thought we were — as I have told this story over the years, I have become anxious about the possibility of overstating our nearness to the bombing. I feel like I owe it to the people who were unlucky enough to be closer to not claim their proximity. Anyway, she agreed with me: about a hundred yards. Like me, she had returned to the spot where we were standing and tried to measure it.

The chute volunteers encouraged us to get moving, away from the finish. William, completely exhausted, his adrenaline draining from his system, was feeling every mile he had just run, and he slowly walked along as best he could. He told me later that he was as alarmed as the rest of us, but, as the enormity of whatever had happened became clearer around us, he mainly started to worry about Ellen, his wife. Where was she? Had she taken advantage of the lateness of the day — the winners and elites had long since finished and were probably showered and dressed by now — to find a premium spot to watch, right by the finish line? Right where the plumes of smoke were?

We heard sirens. One, two, then a lot. The finishing chute volunteers around us looked worried, too, although they were as ignorant as we were. The volunteer coordinators, though, the ones sitting in the high lifeguard chairs to spot runners in trouble or other crises, looked scared. They had radio earpieces. They all waved their arms, shouting, "Keep moving!"

We shuffled through the finish chute, just like you always do at the end of a normal race, so we acted like it was one. Smiling young students looped finishers' medals around our necks. We picked up some bottles of water and Gatorade. We heard more sirens. We might have noticed, if we had turned around, that the flow of runners across the line behind us had stopped. We were the last ones on that day and in that place to do anything normal. In the city, state, and country around us, tweets and texts and news alerts were flashing across everybody's phones, screens, and TVs. The runners on the course, miles back, were being told they couldn't finish the race, but not why. Still in the chute, we had no phones and nobody told us anything, so we continued shuffling along and picked up a granola bar or four. "William," I said as the world around us convulsed in shock and horror, "you want a banana?"

The first moment I knew for certain that something was terribly wrong was when we stepped out of the chute onto Exeter Street and an enormous Boston street cop with a red face and moustache, straight out of a George V. Higgins novel, went sprinting down the street toward the finish line, shouting, "CLEAR THE STREET! CLEAR THE STREET!" He was followed by an ambulance, flashing everything red. "Wow," I said to myself. "What would make that cop run that fast?"

We exited the finishers' area and made our way to the appointed meeting place to find a very worried Josh Warren. "They've stopped the race," he said, telling us that police were holding all the runners still on the course a mile behind the finish line. Which meant, for Josh, that he had up to twenty people scattered along ten miles of pavement, and he had no way of reaching them, because he was holding all of their phones in a plastic bag, and by the way, half of those people were legally blind.

We retrieved our phones from Josh and, like everybody else on the planet, tried to figure out what had just happened; unlike everybody else, we were able to smell it: the air had an acrid tinge, like something had been burned on a pyre. The first thing I saw were texts from friends who knew I was there. "Are you all right?" Twitter said there was an explosion at the Boston Marathon.

Nobody knew what it was. I could not believe it was terrorists. It just seemed so unlikely, the kind of thing my mother would worry about, and I would say, "Mom! Don't be ridiculous!" A woman nearby downloaded a picture of the explosion site. She showed it to me. The sidewalk was covered with a sticky-looking red slick. "Maybe it's Gatorade," I said, far up the denial river.

William was trying to reach Ellen, who was not at the meeting place. The cell towers apparently were overloaded. So I was surprised when my phone rang with a DC area code showing on the screen.

"Peter? This is Julia from *All Things Considered.* We understand you ran the Boston Marathon today?"

I told her I had, and was now standing a few blocks from the finish line.

"Great, yes, apparently there's been a bombing? Could you go on the air and talk to Robert Siegel about it?"

I walked around the corner and back toward the finishing chute while they hooked up a phone line to Robert Siegel in the Washington studio. In the fifteen minutes since we had walked out of it, the finishing chute had been entirely dismantled. Every table and piled crate of bottled water, every banana box, every awning and medical station, gone. The movable fencing that had delineated the chute was still there, though it had all been rearranged to form a perimeter about three blocks east of the finish line.

Robert got on the line. I've known Robert for years, of course, and he's always convivial and joking. Not this time. "Hello, Peter, I understand you're at the finish line? I'm told — yes, we're about to go live, thank you."

Robert has the ability to remain preternaturally calm no matter the circumstances. If we're lucky, we'll have him narrate the apocalypse. The transcript of my one and only contribution to NPR's breaking news coverage follows.

ROBERT SIEGEL: Peter Sagal, the host of the NPR news quiz program *Wait Wait . . . Don't Tell Me!*, ran in the Boston Marathon today, and he joins us now. Peter, how close were you to the explosions?

PETER SAGAL: Robert, I was about a hundred yards beyond the point of the explosion, in what we call the finishing chute. It's a long area that runners walk through after finishing a marathon. We had just finished at about —

I think it was 2:45, around there, Boston time; heard a huge explosion. I had been guiding a blind runner today, so both he and I were shocked. I turned around and saw a big, white plume of smoke that appeared on the other side of the finishing line from us; that is, on the course side. Then another, second large explosion happened just a moment later, with another plume of smoke.

SIEGEL: And did the second explosion come from the same side as the first?

SAGAL: It seemed to. It seemed to come in the same place, from my perspective. At that point, the officials in the marathon asked all of us in the chute to keep moving forward away from it. I've now returned — it's, I guess, twenty minutes, [a] half hour later — to Boylston Street. The chute is completely closed. They're moving people off Boylston Street, and there are no people finishing the race. They seem to have stopped the race. There were many people behind us. Normally, there'd be people flowing through this area by the hundreds, at this point. There's nobody, except for emergency vehicles and police personnel. . . ..

SIEGEL: Can you see if there is a building that has been blown out by an explosion, or where the explosion might have originated?

SAGAL: I'm standing a good three to four hundred yards away. I can see the place where I believe the explosion was. But I cannot, from this distance, see any damage to anything. It's just too far, with too many things in the way. . . .

SIEGEL: And so far, any official description of what happened, or announcement that they're making?

SAGAL: No. I've heard, in just talking to people, I've heard four different rumors, all of which would be irresponsible to share with you because they weren't at all clarified. No official person has made any announcement. Even if they had one, given the chaos and large scale of a postmarathon area, I don't know how we'd hear it. There's no general [PA]. But no, I've been reading my Twitter feed and trying to see the news, just like everybody else has, to find out what happened a hundred yards behind me.

SIEGEL: And Peter, just before you go, once again, the time difference be-

137

tween the two explosions — how quick was that?

SAGAL: Basically, just remembering the moment, heard an explosion, turned around; second explosion. So within . . .

SIEGEL: That quickly.

SAGAL: . . . seconds, yeah.

SIEGEL: Well, Peter Sagal, thank you very much. You're well, I hope. I mean, you didn't get injured . . .

SAGAL: I'm perfectly fine, and I'm very proud to say that I escorted a blind runner, named William Greer, to his first Boston Marathon finish. I'm very proud of that.

Reading this now, I'm both pleased and ashamed that I took the opportunity of a live breaking news hit to brag about my successful guiding. Why didn't I just say, "Hi, Mom!"

I walked back to our meeting place to find that William had been reunited with Ellen, whose face was streaked with tears of relief. I reported in person to my companions what I had just reported to the nation via NPR — that I basically knew nothing — and there, still in an odd bubble of denial and ignorance, though now tinged with apprehension, we said our goodbyes. William and Ellen presented me with a special plaque they had made before the event to thank me for my guiding service. It felt odd to go through with a little ceremony they had planned for a more normal day. We embraced, and went our separate ways to find home.

The whole of Copley Square was blocked off. I walked around it to the west and saw a line of ambulances, dozens of them in a rank, just outside the Fairmont Copley Plaza Hotel. They were obviously there for casualties, and judging by the number of ambulances, they expected a lot of them. News helicopters were swarming overhead. My uncle's house, where I was staying, was about two miles away, back along the course route on Commonwealth Avenue, but as I quickly found out, Commonwealth had been closed, running back for five miles or more. The police were worried there were more bombs along the route, so, forty-five minutes after finishing a marathon, I had to walk a four-mile peregrination through the Fens, until I could get to a place far enough beyond the street closures for my uncle to pick me up.

During that walk, I spoke to Jake Tapper of CNN and Jess Bravin of the *Wall Street*

Journal, and turned down a chance to appear on Glenn Beck's network, TheBlaze. Okay, I didn't just turn down TheBlaze, I told the intermediary who passed on the invite to tell TheBlaze that if I were the last potential guest on earth, and they the last network, that would be the end of the national media. Highlight of the afternoon, actually.

I had to fly to Washington, DC, that night to do an event for the PBS Constitution documentary the next day on Capitol Hill, and I was already so late getting back to my uncle's that I was in danger of missing my flight. I showered and rushed and made calls to the people who were waiting for me in DC, so it was really only when I got to the airport — in plenty of time, as it happened — that I could sit down to open my laptop and start streaming the news.

I learned about Krystle Marie Campbell, Lu Lingzi, and Martin William Richard, all of whom had been killed, and the many others who lost limbs or suffered other terrible injuries. I learned that the bombings occurred at 2:49:43 EDT and 2:49:57 EDT, about thirteen seconds apart (my guess to Robert Siegel was low), while the race clock, marking the elapsed time since the start of our wave, read 4:09. I looked at our finish time, still on my running watch: 4:04. I thought about that. I thought about that a lot, at the airport and on my flight, and in the taxi on the way to my hotel in DC. Once there, I went to the hotel bar, ordered a martini, and read an email from my editor at *Runner's World* asking me to write about the day. I drank off about half the martini in a gulp and wrote down everything that happened, finishing with this:

It only occurred to me, much later, as I viewed online videos of the bombing, how important William's gutsy last mile really was. We crossed the line at 4:04. The bomb went off as the clock read 4:09. Five minutes later. Which might well have been the five minutes that William would have needed to walk those last miserable blocks, had he given in to the urgings of his hip, gut, and mind. But he ran the bravest and toughest mile of his life, not even able to see clearly what he was doing, just because he wanted to be able to say he did it, and by doing so, he crossed the line alive.

I got an email from William the next day, from his home in Austin. He wrote:

I have really sore legs. I am ready to start training for the next marathon, and I'm going to have a lot more long runs. I had the speed, I just need to really increase my endurance. Thanks very much for being my sighted guide; you made the marathon a great pleasure. The only problem[s] were the bombs.

FIVE

My new town house looked, more than anything, like a very big hotel room . . . that is, it appeared as if no one had ever lived there before. All it needed was a minibar and a chocolate on the bedspread every night. It was big and mostly empty — furnished with the unwanted furniture from my former home, and those pieces that were unequivocally mine, like the armchair I won on *Jeopardy!* in 1988 — but felt even emptier. My friend Patti had told me that, as the daughter of divorce herself, the thing that most wounded her was that her father moved into a new home so small it didn't have a room for her, so I was determined to buy myself a large house with rooms for all three of my daughters. Then again, Patti was also my Realtor.

I didn't want a town house, at least not at first, but the houses that Patti showed me in my price range (it was not high, as I knew

I'd still be paying for all my family's expenses, as well as all the legal bills, for the foreseeable future) were weirdly too large. Seeing a place with bedrooms upstairs, and living room and dining room downstairs, it was hard not to imagine myself as a smaller-scale Charles Foster Kane, stumbling at night through empty rooms in my sad isolation. The town house, at least, with its vertical construction, meant that I could avoid wandering through the empty bedrooms simply by ignoring the stairway rising to the next level. Each child would have her own bedroom, on the top floor, with its own bathroom, good for teenage girls.

So now I was "home." I was also hungry. I needed to cook something. But what? And how? And, given my lifelong habit of stress eating, how much of it would I devour? Would this be the place where I finally lapsed into indolence or a second adolescence — same thing — eating dinners of corn chips and beer and frozen taquitos? Would I, a newly divorced dad, become the only worse thing I could think of . . . a fat divorced dad?

"If you've ever been fat, you will either be fat the rest of your life or you will worry about being fat the rest of your life." I came across those words in the manuscript of the play *Fighting International Fat* by Jonathan Reynolds, a pretty obscure place to find the underlying thesis of your waking life, but one doesn't get to specify where one would like it to show up. That casual observation struck me then and now with the profound power of its obvious truth, much like Kafka's observation: "The meaning of life is that it ends." But of course, Kafka did not add that once you're dead, you won't gain weight. Which is a comfort to me, sometimes.

I was, as mentioned earlier, a fat kid, and terribly self-conscious about it, although some of the people who knew me as a child knit their brows in confusion when I tell them this. To them, I might have been a tad chubby, yet well within the bounds of normalcy, but from behind my eyes I was a freak, slow and rubbery and comical, forced to shop in the husky section of the children's clothes store my mother took me to for semiannual bouts of torture. At summer camp I was known as "Pumpkin," which became "Plumpkin," which I accepted at the time as my due, but I felt so ashamed about it inside and thereafter that I kept it a secret from everyone — well, everyone who wasn't at Camp Becket in the mid-1970s — for forty years. Until now. Consider yourself honored.

At the age of fifteen I looked into the mirror and saw somebody I didn't like, so I started to run away from him. I used obsessive running as a way to make my fat self disappear, as quickly as could be managed. I lost almost forty pounds in that first manic bout of running, going from chubby to slender to skinny to thin to my panicked mother bringing me to the doctor. He tested me and found me to be in good shape, if a bit bony — running seven miles a day will do that to you — and told me to be careful I didn't lose too much weight.

I did not tell him that I had been restricting myself to less than one thousand calories a day. I did not tell him how being so hungry all the time takes over your brain. When you're really hungry, as people who fast or are starving due to circumstance will tell you, all you can think about is food. It's why, instead of eating, I would spend the lunch hour at school reading cookbooks in the library. It's why I would turn on the TV and wait through the tedious, meal-less shows for the commercials, hoping they'd be for a restaurant or a packaged food. I yearned to see a film clip of a bowl of steaming Dinty Moore beef stew like most adolescent boys at that time yearned to see a girlie magazine. It's why I would lie in bed at night already tasting the lousy half grapefruit I allowed myself for breakfast.

(Dieting aficionados of a certain age will recognize the half grapefruit for breakfast as a tell for *The Complete Scarsdale Medical Diet,* published by Dr. Herman Tarnower of Scarsdale, New York, which became quite the craze in the late 1970s. Dr. Tarnower, however, is now best remembered for getting himself murdered by a jealous girlfriend around the time I was on the diet in 1980. The late Dr. Tarnower was played by Ben Kingsley in the inevitable movie.)

And for all that fasting and running and denying myself anything, and for all the pounds I shed, I would still take off my shirt at the beginning and end of every day — sometimes I would sneak off to a bathroom with a locked door to do it midday — and look at my protruding ribs and delineated hips and say to myself: "Still too fat."

That breaks my heart, to this day. That the fat kid had transformed himself into what he had always wanted to be: skinny. And he was too crazy to notice it.

I am convinced that although it went undiagnosed at the time I was struggling with a form of anorexia. Research shows there are very few teen boys who starve themselves and waste away to nothing, as anorectic girls do, and those who do tend to be extreme cases. Rather, some boys have the same urge as some girls to destroy themselves through the vehicle of the body, but they do it via extreme exercise. If a boy cuts his calorie count down to eight hundred per day to make weight for wrestling, or if he just obsessively runs long distances, he'll be celebrated for his devotion to bettering himself, even if he wants to better himself right into nothingness. We self-hating teen boys were just another kind of monastic order, down the street from the nunnery, and we chose a different way to flagellate ourselves.

So I dieted obsessively, and I ran a lot. I lost a lot of weight. Becoming a Thin Person after not being one for all of my life was disconcerting, partially because, as said above, I couldn't admit I was actually thin, and also because — surprise — my excess weight wasn't actually the problem. I was the same hot mess, in a smaller bag.

If I were the star of an 80s teen film — or more likely, one of the odder supporting characters — I would have either finally Won the Big Race and celebrated with a big meal, or found a girl Willing to Love Me for Who I Was, and I'd sit down with her to share a sundae as the credits rolled. As it was, this period of my life simply ended, and then I went off to college. There, I couldn't starve myself, because I was too busy: girls; theater; new friends; classes; the challenge, shame, and thrill of finally knowing, beyond any argument or stretch of the imagination or ego, that I wasn't anywhere near the smartest person in the room. I was overwhelmed and delighted and distracted, and what did you know: the dining hall had unlimited refills. It's hard to deny yourself in one area when you're desperate to indulge in all others. And so I gained the weight back, and stopped running for a while, then started again, and ever since then have engaged in the weird war with the mirror: getting fat, getting skinny again, always examining my reflection for more clues as to what I was at any given moment.

As I've related, my late-life running boom started the same way as my first, twenty years before, when I found that there was a lot more of me than I wanted there to be. I started running again. I ran a race, and then I became determined to do a marathon, and I did, and then another, and I became a serious runner, and I lost thirty pounds along the way, and I'll be damned if I gain them back.

Or should I say: more damned. Because the obsession with weight, far more common among male amateur athletes than you might suppose, is a kind of curse. "I run to eat," we say, and this is true, but we're not so much taking pleasure in the food as in the immunity our running gives us. We hit the box of doughnuts at work or the side of fries with lunch, saying to ourselves, "I did my six this morning," and feel, for a fleeting moment, that We Are Like Everybody Else, somebody who can indulge in sweets and fats without exposing ourselves as freaks.

Being overweight in and of itself isn't the issue. I know people of all shapes and I have learned that their sense of self isn't in any way determined by how much they weigh, although it is often the case that they are deeply affected by society's veneration of the thin and rejection of those who are not. It is, for some of us, simply the internalized horror of what we might become if we allow ourselves to get weak, to let go, to slow down.

You should not run simply to lose weight, although if you do run, you probably will. There are a number of excellent reasons why you might not drop many pounds — one of which is that depending on how much you weigh now, and your history and your biology (far beyond the simple chemical transactions we call "metabolism") and your age, you may not even need to lose weight. Bodies are different, and research has shown that different people have different "set points," a weight that you settle into as your point of equilibrium, even if it's ten pounds more than a similar person of similar build and height. Another is that by becoming fit, you will build muscle, replacing one kind of weight with another. But most importantly: that way madness lies. To obsess about weight is to abject yourself before the god of the bathroom scale, to try to placate its obscure will, to take its praise as Gospel and its disapproval as damnation.

If you do, through some combination of circumstance or extraordinary self-discipline or madness — such as my high school bout of protoanorexia — manage to lose weight below your "set point," your body will let you know, by possessing your brain in the manner of a demon of hunger. Everybody knows the feeling of their thoughts straying toward dinner as the day goes along . . . you start to get peckish about four, and before you even realize you're hungry you think that maybe tonight you'll stop at that good Chinese takeout place on the way home, or remember there are still some

151

chicken thighs in the fridge you can fry up. Now, take that happy anticipatory peckish musing and give it methamphetamine. Just as I did during my hermitage in high school, you'll obsessively focus on your next meal, whatever it is you allow yourself, and once it arrives you will gobble it up and end up licking the bowl like a starved dog, and then start thinking about whatever meal is next, and that will continue until you gain the weight back.

And don't even get me started on the body mass index (BMI). Under that rubric, even at my fittest, when I could reel off seven-minute miles one after another for ten miles or more, I was still officially overweight. Your fitness is not reflected in your appearance. Watch a track and field competition — there will be an array of bodies, from the tiny, slender long-distance runners to the broad-shouldered and heavy discus throwers. Each of them is a superb athlete and very, very few of them will ever end up on the cover of *Men's Fitness* or *Shape* with their shirt and/or pants off. Health has a thousand ways of expressing itself, and the least important way is how much fat you can pinch between your fingers.

Running has exploded in popularity in the

last decade, and it's hard not to correlate the sport's growth with the obesity crisis. People feel fat, people are fat, people are terrified of getting fat, and then they see ridiculously fit people in spandex on the cover of *Runner's World,* leaping through the blank Pantone background like gods and goddesses descending from heaven, saying, Why not give this running thing a try?

If you read about the cover subjects in the note inside the magazine, you will discover that many of them aren't actually runners but general-purpose fitness models, gifted with genetics, youth, and the ability to spend hours every day in the gym and get paid for it. Real pro runners — the kind of people who become famous by simply being very good at running — are too skinny. Readers don't want to become a bony ectomorph with the gaunt, haunted look of a hunted elk. They want to become muscular, smooth, handsome/beautiful, with perfect skin and not a single hair — perhaps blown off by the rushing wind as they lope through the California sun. You can run to Zanzibar and never find that person looking back at you from a mirror. Recently, though, the magazine has been featuring "real runners" on their cover, although, strangely, not me. Yet.

That said: physics applies to runners as well. To move a certain mass, you need a certain amount of energy. Most runners lose weight not simply because of the increased caloric expenditure, but because the body has a natural ability to adapt to whatever its purpose becomes. People who lift heavy things become bigger, thicker, more stable; people who move quickly and constantly become smaller, lighter, sharper, with less excess to drag along. The elite runners I've met look narrow and sharp, carved out of flat planes that cut through the air, like a stealth bomber.

That probably will never happen to you, just as it never happened to me — even when I was in my top running shape, I was still short and squat, and I will die with the love handles I was born with. What can happen, though, is a transformation of your body, not just a loss of fat and gain of muscle, but a metamorphosis of body and mind. If you can pass through that difficult initial period, and become somebody who runs four or five times a week, you can increase your average daily caloric expenditure by a third or more. If you manage not to give in to the common urge to "reward" yourself for your run with an extra cupcake, the weight will come off naturally, and over time your set point, your body's own equilibrium, will start to change.

If you keep it up, running will help you become not the person you see on the magazine covers but yourself, or at least a version of you closer to what evolution designed you to be. Chances are, you weren't designed to be a fitness model. But evolution certainly didn't mean for you to sit on a couch. You were designed over millions of years to chase your food across the veldt, or at least to flee from something trying to do the same to you, and by returning to that initial purpose, you can restore your own primordial form. Our premodern ancestors were in excellent shape, Fred Flintstone notwithstanding.

One thing that will help of course is diet, and that too, is something your running will affect, and something that will affect your running. By diet, I mean what you actually eat, not what some magazine or author or murdered doctor or celebrity or wife of Jerry Seinfeld recommends you should eat. That kind of diet doesn't work, and never has, and never will. The secret of every single diet is calorie restriction, imposed by various kinds of gimmicks, be it all carbs or all fats or all things we assume our ancient ancestors would have eaten in their healthy natural lifestyles, right up until the moment they themselves were eaten by a bear at the age of thirty.

The reason my lunchtime sojourns to the library worked — if making me skinny yet miserable can be called "working" — is that, like all diets ever invented, they restricted my calories. If you consume fewer calories than you expend, like, say, via obsessive running, you will lose weight as the body makes up the difference by breaking down stored fat. Here: I just invented the Second File Cabinet Diet, in which you eat only foods starting with the letters M–Z. Marshmallows, but no apples. Try it and you'll lose weight, for a while, until you go mad and gorge yourself on figs.

In 2010, Professor Mark Haub of Kansas State University decided to prove this point by putting himself on a diet of only Twinkies and other processed snack foods. His intent was to see if only restricting calories (in his case, down to 1,800 calories a day) was sufficient to lose weight, without any regard for the kinds of foods those calories came in. His results were impressive, and would be the kind of thing that could have made him into a diet guru were he a minor celebrity: he lost twenty-seven pounds in two months, with no negative effects on his health at all. Unfortunately for his future career as the Twinkie Diet Millionaire, he's a scientist, so he was actually kind of glum about his findings: "I wish I could say it's healthy. I'm not confident enough in doing that."

So what is a weight-obsessed runner to do in order to lose weight and keep it off, if not diet? It's simple. Make sure as much of your diet as possible is "clean" food — non-processed, and raw when you buy it. Buy what you need when you need it, the way Europeans do, so your food won't sit long enough in your house to need preservatives or stabilizers. Avoid things with colorful packaging and lists of ingredients in tiny type, especially if they're words you can't pronounce.

Carbs are fine, as long as they come in the form of vegetables and fruits and natural starches. Protein is fine, as long as it comes in beans, legumes, and leaner, nonprocessed meats. Even fat is fine, as long as it comes in natural oils and in the fruits and meats that contain them. Food is processed so as to maximize the things we like about food — sugars, fats — and eliminate things like bitter flavors and fiber, which normally serve to keep us from eating too much. We have evolved over millions of years to be natural omnivores, but it will take another million to adapt to eating Cheetos.

And, of course, if you can, cook your own food. And everybody can.

Most of the things people tend to buy premade, be they hamburger patties or pancake mix, are ridiculously easy to prepare yourself, and taste much better when you do. A hamburger? Buy fresh ground beef, sprinkle with salt and pepper, shape it loosely into a patty, and fry it in its own fat in a hot cast iron pan. Pancake? Flour, salt, baking powder, sugar, milk, eggs, butter. The food you make at home will generally be fresher, less processed, and thus less caloric than what you buy premade at a store or in a restaurant. Plus, if you bake your own bread, you'll know for a fact you didn't slip in any high-fructose corn syrup, unless you have a split personality and your other self is trying to kill you.

One of the great mental obstacles to home cooking is current food culture, which revolves around TV shows depicting tense protogeniuses trying to whip alchemical cuisine out of things like old rutabagas and shredded tires. They apply sous vide cookers and pastry bags and nitrogen injectors to create foams and curls and reclaimed reductions, so we begin to think of cooking as something impossibly complicated, something best watched rather than attempted. As writer Michael Pollan noted in 2009, the rise of cooking shows — or more aptly, food shows — coincided with a decline of home cooking.

But if you think of the things you actually like to eat, rather than watch being prepared — be it a burger, or vegetarian chili, or a grilled cheese sandwich — they are all simple. And as such, they are not guilty pleasures — they are merely pleasures, and easily recreated at will.

During most of my deceased marriage, my wife had stayed home to take care of the children, and thus had done almost all of the cooking. She had been raised by a mother and aunts who had learned to cook from their mothers and aunts, and she knew all these alchemical tricks, like how to make a white sauce or how to cut onions so that they flavored a dish rather than interrupted it with rubbery chunks, as when I cooked with them. She proudly never followed a recipe exactly — always adding or subtracting something — and while it's hard to say whether her results were better than the exact recipe might have been, they were always good. She was showing off, and justifiably so.

As for me, I was in charge of the Dad Foods. I did all the grilling and specialized in anything that required cool equipment, like the electric crepe maker. But my approach to cooking was algorithmic. A recipe (or the instructions on the electric crepe maker) was a series of steps to be followed, and if the result didn't come out well, it was probably because I didn't follow the steps correctly. When making food for the kids, I didn't dare second-guess the instructions as their mother could. I didn't know how to do anything but follow directions. If there were no directions, I was at a loss. Which, come to think of it, might be part of the reason I ended up alone in this town house.

But even if I had taken an unexpected off-ramp into Divorceland, I didn't have to do everything this particular script required. I wasn't going to become one of those divorced men whose refrigerators were filled with nothing but half-empty takeout containers, with a pile of soy sauce packets in the butter compartment. I was going to learn to cook. From scratch. Raw ingredients, to be used by a raw cook.

In the years since those first nights, I've learned to make decent home-cooked food. I did it through practice, and tasting what I was cooking while I was cooking it, and using recipes not just as instructions but as lessons. If a recipe told me to add something, I tried to figure out why. When I could, I'd taste something before adding an additional ingredient and then after to see what improvement it had made. I can now make a good white sauce of my own, and a wine reduction, and I can (finally) do wonders with an onion and a sharp knife. But mostly, I learned this: The secret to eating well is simply to eat well, meaning ingredients you can identify prepared in a way replicable by you in your own kitchen. The secret to not eating too much is to stop eating when you're not hungry anymore. The secret of a good diet is to cook and the secret of cooking is to care, about the food you're making, about the ingredients you're using, and mostly about the person you're cooking for, especially if that person is yourself. Back in high school, I waged war on my own body and my own desires, and to hate your desires is to hate yourself. These days, me and I get along much better. Sure, I could stand to lose a little weight, but I'm healthy for my age, I can still reel off a fast ten miles if I need do, and afterward I can cook you a pretty good meal.

Here's the other thing I've learned, which is something everyone used to know, something I knew even while manning the hamburger grill: food is love. To cook for yourself, rather than merely feed yourself, is to show yourself love, especially important when there is a sudden and marked lack of others willing to do that. To cook for others is not only a form of caring, it's a form of connection. The transformation of raw ingredients into cuisine is often called alchemy, but the true alchemy is what happens to you, the people you cook for, and the relationship between all of you.

But all of that was in front of me on that May evening in 2013. I looked in my refrigerator. I took out some freshly purchased onions, peppers, mushrooms, and jarred garlic. I sautéed them in oil while I boiled Asian noodles in a pot. Once the vegetables were cooked, I doused them with soy sauce (way too much this time; I eventually learned to use less soy, which is mostly salt, and combine it with ginger and chili oil and a little fish sauce for umami). Then the noodles were drained and mixed in with the vegetables. I put the whole thing in a bowl and set it down on my table.

This particular table was an old, worn IKEA laminated pine kitchen table from my former home, one that got stored rather than thrown out when it was replaced because our family had once spent an evening decorating it with painted pictures of our place settings, surrounded by our names. Five places, each with a tempera paint illustration of a favorite meal, done in styles that befit our ages and talent, "Mama" and "Papa" and the names of our three children, all frozen in a moment of greater happiness, some six years before. It was one of the old pieces of furniture I was delighted to claim. So, on my first night living alone, I sat at my place, marked "Papa," and ate my meal, on the souvenir of my family.

Six

Sometimes running sucks.

This is not something most runners talk about in public, though it is something runners talk to one another about all the time, usually during another, different run, to pass the time pleasantly so this run won't suck as much as the one they're talking about. No evangelical warns converts about boring sermons; no Mormon missionary loosens his narrow black tie and says, "Truth be told, there are days I would murder someone for a cup of coffee." We're trying to persuade you to buy into a lifestyle, and the secret to sales is to let the customer discover the defects in your product on her own, once it's too late.

But I wasn't cut out to be a salesman. I am terrible at being cheerful, and at denying obvious flaws. I am a bipedal Eeyore. Were I unfortunate enough to have ended up selling cars for a living, every American would be reaching every destination on foot, and this book would be unnecessary.

So let me be honest: sometimes there is no "runner's high," no being one with the environment, no fellowship with fellow fellows, no leisurely loping through the lea. Sometimes there are aches and pains and headaches and light-headedness, sometimes your feet hurt, and sometimes your feet are the only things that don't hurt. Many, many people tell me that they tried running once and hated it. And I say, "Well, give it a little more time," and then they do and come back and say, "Now I hate it for a longer period of time."

In my running career I have aggravated my piriformis nerve and ended up spending six weeks with a physical therapist. I have slipped on a sheet of ice and landed so hard on my back I saw stars on a clear winter day. I've twisted ankles, pulled muscles in my hips, back, and somehow even my neck. During the New York City Marathon in 2009, my calves were cramping so badly during the last five miles that I made a deal with myself: I would keep running until I actually screamed, and only then would I take a break, which turned out to be, on average, once every quarter mile. Earlier the same year, after qualifying to run the Boston

Marathon (again) and training up to run it, I was also coaching my daughter's T-ball team. One day during practice I turned to point out the location of third base (these little girls were unclear on the concept) and felt what I thought was a softball ricocheting off my lower leg, resulting in an audible "pop." I turned around and looked to see who had thrown the ball. There was no ball. I had ruptured a tendon. Instead of going to Boston, I went back to the physical therapist, who greeted me with a warm smile. She had missed me.

As I aggressively trained to be a serious runner, for the roughly five years that began with my training for the 2006 Chicago Marathon, I decided that I must embrace the pain. "What does not kill us makes us stronger," I muttered as I tried to get a footing on the ice during a 5-degree winter run. "Pain is weakness leaving the body," I said to myself, as a mantra, as I tried to keep up with my friends on a 4 × 800-meter track workout. And as for races, I ran them according to the rule laid out by a famous miler decades ago: "The perfect mile race is one in which you lose consciousness just on the other side of the finish line." If that was true, then the 2007 Rock 'n' Roll Chicago Half Marathon was as close to perfect as I was going to attain in this fallen world, because I pushed myself, gasping air through gritted teeth, ignoring the protests of every muscle in my body, to set a PR of 1:28, and then I collapsed to the ground. If there had been a coffin available, I would have gratefully laid down inside it.

Because, although we don't like to admit it, pain is enjoyable, especially in a world in which physical pain — even the mild burn one feels during physical exertion — is, for most people and for the most part, completely avoidable. There is no real need to push oneself to the point of discomfort in a world of cars and helpful machines, and even if you do choose to exercise, there is no reason to endure the elements with year-round climate control and twenty-four-hour gyms, with their elliptical machines so you don't put any stress on your joints and built-in TVs so you won't be bored. And, of course, almost any physical pain can be managed by a wide array of medications, often to our detriment. Thus, many of us weekend warriors are out there looking to suffer, probably to prove to ourselves we can. After a particularly tough Chicago Marathon one year, I stumbled up the steps of my home, carefully navigating each riser, and my then wife asked, "Why do you do it if it hurts so much?" I responded, "That's kind of the point."

Among the most popular kinds of races these days are the Tough Mudder or Spartan Races, a dozen different variants on the same test-your-mettle theme: get yourself out of your office, and out of your luxury gym with its fresh juice bar, and get down into the mud and run through the flames, and make yourself wet and miserable and possibly even injured, and pay money to do it, because when you're done, and you've experienced something really uncomfortable, well, then, at least you'll know you're alive. It's the mantra of CrossFit and boot camps and ultra-long-distance bike racing, like the Race Across America, where competitors say they look forward to the hallucinations because at least they're entertaining. Get out there! Punish yourself! Feel something! Sometimes pain seems like the only solution to a general numbing.

This obsession became mine in those early years, and I prided myself on how much I could take. To be fast and good meant to be tough and strong, and to be tough and strong meant to be able to endure pain. So, yes, of course running sucked. The trick is, as Lawrence of Arabia put it, not to mind. Which worked fine, for me, until one day —

as movie villains like to say — I learned the true meaning of pain.

I have always secretly hoped that if I someday found myself lying on the ground gasping for breath, gravely injured, perhaps fatally, I would come up with something really great to say. Some declaration of immortal love, perhaps, or wisdom for my children, or at least something witty. As it happened, when it happened, the best I could do was a whimper, and when the first witness to my accident came running up, I grunted "Could you call 911, please?" I was proud of the "please." Not memorable but at least polite.

It was a beautiful summer day, a Wednesday, August 11, 2010, and as it was an off day from running I had to decide between a swim and a bike ride, either useful for my upcoming triathlon. Wednesdays were usually swimming days during that summer, but it had been a while since I'd been out on the bike. I had missed the 6 AM departure of the group ride, but what the hell — I had just begun two weeks off from work, so I decided to go out by myself, with the same cheery nonchalance with which Archduke Franz Ferdinand once decided to take a trip around Sarajevo in an open car.

I approached the intersection at a decent clip, noting the car arriving from the right, an orange hatchback, slowing at the stop sign, certain that — as had happened every single time before in my biking career — the driver would see me and let me pass before pulling into the intersection. But she did not, and we arrived at the same spot in the center of the intersection at the same moment. Time did not, as the cliché has it, slow down as the car accelerated into my path. It all happened at normal speed, giving me enough time to shout "Stop! Stop!" but not enough for either of us to do so. The impacts — first with the car, then with the car again as I descended from my short trip upward, and then with the ground — hurt, as expectations and the laws of physics would predict. My head slammed into the pavement, cracking my helmet, which thus saved my skull and perhaps my life. I lay on the ground, curled fetally on my side, struggling to breathe, thinking, "Oh my God, I was just hit by a car," just the way Woody whispers "I'm a lost toy!" in *Toy Story:* that is, an awful event that I had always heard about happening to the unluckiest and unwisest of people had now happened to me, making me one of them.

By the time the ambulance arrived at the

scene I was beginning to think I might have escaped with no serious injuries. My breath was coming easier and I could wiggle my toes and move my arms, although I hadn't yet dared to try to get up. The paramedics checked me thoroughly — for injuries to my extremities, for bleeding, for signs of a concussion — and found nothing. One of them said, in a rather formal way, "It seems as if you have just had the breath knocked out of you. We could take you to the hospital, if you request that, or perhaps . . . you would just like to go home." I immediately started to feel bad for wasting everybody's time. "Let me get up and see if I can shake this off," I said, and for the first time since the impact, tried to sit up. Just then, an invisible angry dwarf stabbed me in the back with a spear made of molten lava, the worst pain I have ever felt in my life, and I screamed, and froze, too terrified to continue getting up, or to lay back down, or do anything, ever again.

The ride to the hospital — strapped into the stretcher, head immobilized — the triage at the emergency room, and trips to the X-ray and CT scan rooms all happened in a blur of changing ceilings. I felt fine, in no pain whatsoever, as long as I remained flat on my back. If I tried to sit up or twist or roll to the slightest degree, the angry dwarf stabbed me again, so I stayed flat, and enjoyed the Dilaudid, until I got my diagnosis.

"There's nothing wrong with you. Nothing [is] broken," said the trauma doctor.

"Then why does it hurt so much when I try to move?"

"Deep bruising," he said, and shrugged.

I believed him because he was a doctor and I was a guy in spandex bike shorts who whimpered like a puppy every time I tried to sit up. They checked me into the hospital and started me on a morphine drip, thinking — I supposed — that I was just a little bit delicate and needed some meds to stop my whining. The next three days passed in a morphine haze, punctuated by meals I didn't particularly want, visits from my wife and children I don't remember, and a dose of Valium that made me even less interested in doing anything other than watching the ceiling stay still for a change. It was during that Valium-induced nap that the call came — a call I was too drugged to answer, and thus spent a good six hours trying futilely to return — explaining to me that hey, now: they had found something on the CT scans after all.

"The good news is, we don't have to operate, it'll just heal," said the cheerful neuro-surgeon who stopped by to see me the next day, after I had woken up. "The bad news is it's going to hurt a lot, for a couple of weeks, then hurt a bit for six weeks, and then you'll be fine."

Picture a vertebra. There is the main structure, round and hollow like a napkin ring, down the middle of which runs the spinal column. Jutting off it to the sides are bony extensions called "transverse pro-cesses," which provide an anchor point for a whole bunch of interesting muscles run-ning through your side and back. I had managed to snap off two transverse pro-cesses on my left side, low down. Which, as it turns out, was why trying to move kept making me scream.

Four days after the accident they wheeled me out of the hospital and my wife helped me, gingerly, into our car, and took me directly to the supermarket to drop off my prescription of painkillers and then wait for it to be filled. I didn't want to sit in the car by myself, so instead I wobbled painfully into the store, where the only place to sit was on one of those electric scooters elderly people use to shop. There was no key, and there was no rule against it, so I celebrated my release by cruising around the supermarket in an electric scooter, trying to cultivate the look of someone used to greater speeds.

The problem with being immobile is you can't move. During the first week of my recuperation, my family took a planned beach vacation in Wisconsin, and I kept trying to do insane extreme sports, like standing up from chairs, rolling over in bed, and even walking. I found that if I held my back in a certain way — as if I was cocking my hip provocatively at some imaginary sailors — it could keep the painful spasms at bay, but doing so began to strain the rest of my back. My lowest moment came at the end of a half-mile shuffle on the beach, during which I kept having to bend doubled over to relieve the ache in my back, and I eventually had to send my poor wife hurrying back to the house to fetch the car, while my daughters held my hand and cooed comfort.

"I run marathons," I muttered under my breath. "This isn't me."

But it was. This was a different category than my pulls and strains, even the time I tore my calf tendon. Those were training injuries, proof that I was hard-core, and a few weeks or even months of changing my workout routine was a small price to pay for such a badge of badassery. But now I felt utterly useless, and cut off entirely from any kind of training, which for years had been my refuge, my pride, and my natural anti-depressant. I was sliding down into a spiral of gloom, and I spent the rest of the vacation sitting in a chair on the beach, looking out at the water, like the paralyzed hero in *The Diving Bell and the Butterfly,* waiting for someone to wheel me back in.

The next week, though, I was feeling well enough to visit the doctor, and I got the okay to begin — lightly, gently, carefully — exercising again. I went to the gym, lowered myself into a recumbent stationary bike, and moved my legs without pain for the first time in weeks, desperately lapping up the faint fumes of endorphins like an alcoholic licking a bottle. I managed twenty minutes before my back started to bark at me, and I felt torn . . . on the one hand, I was thrilled to have actually broken a sweat because of something other than terror or anxiety, but on the other, I felt pathetic and small. Perhaps next time I'd use the handbike, after making myself feel better about my weakness and fragility by bumping the senior citizen currently using it to the floor.

It was late August. I wrote off the Chicago Triathlon at the end of the month as too great a risk of death by drowning. However, I had registered for the Chicago Marathon six weeks later, on October 10, 2010 (10/10/10), and I was determined to be there on the starting line. This struck those who didn't know me well as crazy, and those who did know me well as crazier than usual. I had been hit by a car, hard enough to leave large, me-shaped dents in the sheet metal, and I was talking about running twenty-six miles not two months later. I realized they were right, so I stopped talking about it.

For my first run after the accident, I went out alone. I didn't know what would happen, or what would break, and didn't think any of the options might be pretty. I stepped softly and slowly, as if I were learning to walk, and managed three miles before my back started to stiffen. I felt both excited and depressed: I was running again, but running as if I had never run before.

And so it was for the month of September. My running was slow, painful, and it seemed that in the four weeks of complete and near immobility after the accident I had lost four months' worth of fitness and gained four years in age. I felt fragile and vulnerable and ceded my usual place near the front of my running group, following along from the back, shrieking out warnings whenever a car approached anywhere near an intersection.

The day of the 2010 Chicago Marathon approached. The idea of walking away from another race seemed like one defeat too many, so I decided to do it. I stumbled painfully through some longer runs, ending up bent over and gasping each time. Six days before the marathon, I did a short run with the editor of *Runner's World,* David Willey, and afterward he looked me up and down, and he said, "You'll do fine. Everybody who gets laid up with an injury does great at races after they recover, because they had enforced rest." This seemed insane to me. I had lost so much time, and so much speed, and so much fitness, that I still had no idea if I could even finish the race.

At 7:25 AM, on the tenth of October, in Grant Park in Chicago, I stood in a seeded corral that had been earned, it seemed to me, in another lifetime. My right knee felt creaky and gritty, like somebody had forgotten to oil it. I was tired and dulled and still a bit hungover from a successful series of performances (and after-parties) with my radio show the prior week in New York City. Then the crowd around me started to shuffle forward with a cheer, and I started to move my legs forward, and swing my arms, and I committed myself to the road.

My plan was to help pace a friend to his 3:30 Boston qualifier, keep it up as long as I could, and give him a cheerful wave and a pat on the back when I flagged, which I anticipated would be around the ten-mile mark. But by the five-mile marker I had left him behind. Keeping to a 7:50 pace seemed surprisingly easy. I expected nothing except to fail, so I kept going until I did, and when I didn't, I kept going. The familiar landmarks slipped by . . . downtown, Lincoln Park, Boystown, downtown again, Little Italy. I kept waiting for the inevitable, and it never happened. My back felt fine. My legs felt fine. I kept running.

The heat rose and I flagged a bit in the last four miles, stopping to douse my head and slurp down fluids, but still, no disasters, no breakdowns, and no pain. I climbed the course's one hill at Roosevelt Road and turned and went down the gauntlet of the finishing chute, not sprinting, not giving up, just waiting, again, for something to stop me. The simplest pleasure is to move, so I just moved.

My watch read 3:27, my third fastest marathon ever, a Boston qualifier, and without question, my easiest and most pleasurable 26.2. Even as the inevitable cramps and soreness started postrace, as the blood rushed to the strained muscles in my legs, I still felt elated. I thought of an old story about a samurai who went into a duel with a perfect resignation, prepared to die, and his opponent, frightened by his calm, withdrew from the duel. I had entered the race expecting the worst, and the worst had never come. In fact, one could argue, it was my best race ever.

I strolled out of the finishers' chute with my friends, who, having pressed and tried to do their best, had either exhausted themselves or collapsed completely, and thought about where I had been two months before: lying on the ground, with broken bones in my back, gasping for breath and wondering if I would ever move again. I walked out of the park to Michigan Avenue and stopped at the crosswalk, and carefully looked at the drivers of the cars stopped at the light, and gave them a wave to make sure they noticed that I was moving.

I was so pleased with myself. I thought I had run through, truly, the valley of the shadow of death, and emerged unscathed on the other side. And I had! But not completely.

It was an October morning, three years after

that race in 2010. I woke up at 7 AM in my Divorced Dad Town House, having missed my running group's early morning start. Again. Dammit. I had expected that with no kids to look after, I would be able to devote even more time to running. But going running at six in the morning — or earlier — only makes sense if there's an important reason to be back home at seven. Now that I was no longer responsible for waking my kids at that hour, or feeding them, or sending them off to school — lucky me — it was harder to justify going to bed early enough to wake up at five thirty to be out on the street by six, and since I wasn't going to go to bed early anyway, I might as well mix myself another drink, and what's that you say, Netflix? Another episode of *Parks and Recreation* will start in just fifteen seconds? Who am I to say no? I got nobody else but you, Netflix.

I picked a shirt from the basket that wasn't that smelly, added shorts and shoes, and headed out the door. I made it exactly one mile before I ran into the grocery store.

Once inside, I didn't need to ask directions; I had scouted this place out months before. And I certainly wasn't going to waste time asking permission. Across the store diagonally — damn, why did it have to be all the way on the far side — through a big swinging door into the storage area, right turn, down some stairs, through the employee break room — look, motivational posters, how precious — and straight to the gray door. Anybody watching me traverse those last fifteen feet would have seen a man skewered between the need to hurry and the need not to jostle any systems, as if he were wearing a motion-sensitive bomb vest. And I was, sort of. At least, there was a risk of explosion.

Proximity to the target has a strange effect on the mind-body system, and with every step toward my destination my need to already be there became more acute. I might have leaped the last few feet. I may not have locked the door. And then . . .

The first thing we're going to need is a euphemism. Something evocative but not gross, something original so it doesn't bring up past unpleasantness. How about "egress," a lovely antique word with the simple meaning "to exit." Done. Egress.

As I said, when I was brought to the hospital after being hit by the Orange Nissan of Death, the helpful nurses put me on morphine to ease my considerable pain. Opioids have a lot of wonderful effects, but they often paralyze the digestive tract. Thus,

I did not egress for four or five days, although I was too blissed out to care. (This is apparently a common side effect of opioids, judging from the ads for "opioid-induced constipation" medications I see on cable TV.)

Since then, though, and up until this very day, my running career has been punctuated by what some call "cramps," although those can get confused with the muscular kind. Others call this phenomenon "the trots," but technically, most runners trot every now and then, especially after a speed workout. And of course there's "the runs," but that's a distressingly confusing homonym. But this is something very particular, and something very, very hard to ignore. It is nothing so much as a specific subassembly of the bodily machinery taking over from the brain and insisting on having its own way. You may not want to stop; you may be in the midst of a race or a large group run. You may not have any place to stop. But you will stop, or you will explode. The Egress will not be denied.

So in recent years I have found myself hunkered down in bushes and alleys, hoping I won't be discovered, arrested, or shot. I have made my poor running buddies wait up to three times during a long run while I inspect the inside of some construction site's porta-potty or a Starbucks restroom. I squandered the one real chance I've ever had to win a race — that 5K in Hamilton, New York, two days before the 2013 Boston Marathon — because I had to duck into the woods and find a secluded spot. While I egressed, two runners passed me. I came in third.

Conventional wisdom suggests first to look at the other end of the system — what are you eating, and when are you eating it? But that seems to have nothing to do with it. It doesn't matter what I eat the night before and it doesn't matter when I eat it. (I never eat within an hour of going for a run, and I never eat at all before a morning run.) The other solution, obviously, is to get up a little early, move around, and then spend some time egressing in the warm privacy of my own house. I've tried it. It doesn't work; whatever I do, within a few miles, the gremlin awakes. My body (or, a specific section of my body) apparently needs me to run a mile or two before it's ready to work. I've even tried going for a mile jog and then returning home, to see if I can fool my system into thinking I've started my actual run — nothing. My body seems to know when I'm actually running and when I'm just pretending.

All this has led me to have a very strange relationship with my own digestive system — as if it's another being who happens to be occupying the same body as the rest of me. We get along, in a mostly symbiotic relationship — like those birds who clean the teeth of crocodiles. But eventually we disagree. I have even had conversations with my gut — once, running along a familiar beach in Massachusetts, near my parents' home, my large intestine let me know it would like to make a stop. I told it not to worry, there was a public restroom up ahead. When we arrived, the restroom was locked. I told my gut it would have to wait. My gut was having none of it. I spent the next two days worried that the *Boston Globe* would run a headline, "Public radio host found lurking in bushes, doing unspeakable things."

Fed up with this constant interruption, I consulted an expert. Dr. Satish Rao is a (intake of breath) professor of medicine and the chief of section on gastroenterology and hepatology and director of the Digestive Health Center at Augusta University in Georgia and thus, as Gene Weingarten of the *Washington Post* put it, "the greatest living American expert in the field of how poop moves through the body."

In his pursuit of colonic knowledge, and specifically of how exercise affects the "motility of material" within the colon, Dr. Rao once asked healthy test subjects to exercise at up to 90 percent of capacity with probes inserted into their behinds. I assumed these were tiny things, like suppositories or maybe one of those buglike things from *The Matrix*. "Oh, no," said Dr. Rao, who, perhaps as a survival technique, has maintained his sense of humor about his subject. "The colon is about three feet long! We use a three-and-a-half-foot-long tube!"

So these men and women ran as best they could — what does a three-and-a-half-foot tube up your business do to your stride? — and Dr. Rao discovered a strange and unexpected thing: during intense exercise, the colon "goes quiet." "In fact," he told me, "the higher intensity of the exercise, the quieter the colon became." His hypothesis is that blood rushes away from the colon to support the other systems involved in exercise — muscles, heart, lungs — and the colon, starved of energy, hibernates.

At the same time, those porta-potties don't line marathon routes for the comfort of the spectators. Dr. Rao doesn't know for sure, as we "don't have the technology yet" to figure it out — the mind boggles at the thought of even bigger probes — but his guess is that after a long while of being starved of oxygen, the colon might "complain" by cramping, in the same way that the sharp chest pains known as angina are caused by a lack of blood to the heart. And, he says, once exercise stops, the colon wakes up with a vengeance. Your colon cramps up, you stop because of the pain, and the machinery whirrs back to life, sending you to a porta-potty or behind the nearest bush.

But what about me? It's no longer an occasional disaster; it's a regular part of my runs, as much as tying my shoes or starting my watch. Dr. Rao believes that my situation was related to my accident, but not quite in the way I imagined. His theory is that my injury to my vertebrae might have affected the nerves running down to the business end of my GI tract. Which, in turn, might have affected the complex interactions that take place down there — the dance of the colon, as it were.

First, he suggested trying an over-the-counter probiotic. More and more research shows that the bacteria of the gut contributes to its well-ordered functioning, so why not go to Whole Foods and pay twenty bucks for a jar of the stuff? (Other doctors are experimenting with fecal transplants. To which I say: THANK YOU, BUT NO.) Perhaps a dose of store-bought bacteria would restore my intestinal flora to the lovely garden of germs they were before the accident. If that didn't work, he suggested I try a prescription medication that would help reabsorb bile, if any extra was sloshing around where it shouldn't be. I tried the probiotic, and there was no effect, which I guess is what you'd expect when you throw down a bunch of randomly selected bacteria into your gut in the hope that it will do some good.

So, where once I was a runner who pointed my nose at the horizon, now I am one that sketches a dot-to-dot around the map, from restaurant restroom (God bless you, McDonald's) to construction site porta-potty to grocery store. If I am anywhere within four miles of my home, I know where every public restroom is and what gyrations need to be accomplished to get to it, be it walking by a counter or daring the anger of a security guard. Here at the grocery store, nobody seemed to care. Larger institutions were often the best; since there were so many employees, it fell to no one to do anything about the sweaty, stressed bald man walking purposefully through the stockroom. Although, to be fair, the look on my face — a combination of determination, panic, and agony — was such that I don't think anybody would dare mess with me.

Egress accomplished, emergency abated, I strolled more casually (but still purposefully, for camouflage purposes) back toward the exit. I hoped that every clerk was far too focused on refilling the dairy case to care about my walking in and out without buying anything, or my appearance, or my smell. I was right, at least this time. Once outside, I started running again, headed south, where I knew there was a twenty-four-hour Laundromat waiting, if necessary. Or, when.

SEVEN

I looked around the picnic tables, and only about half the audience looked back at me. The rest were staring into space or at the ground or somewhere I'm not even sure they knew. I kept talking anyway.

"So William and I were only about a hundred yards away when we heard a huge boom!"

Some of the kids flinched. Some of them marveled. A few of them grinned but still didn't look at me. I didn't worry they were bored. On this September night I was (once again) telling the story of the Boston Marathon, from five months earlier, and how William Greer had gutted out that last mile, possibly saving us from being caught in the terrorist bombing.

"I know he saved your life!" cried Luke, who was ten years old. "He knew the bomb was there! He just knew! And that's why he ran! Because he knew!"

"You think so?" I asked.

"What's a bomb?" asked Amar, nine.

Luke and Amar and all the other children around me, dressed in pale green knit shirts and light khaki shorts, were residents at the Louisiana School for the Visually Impaired, and they were gathered for their evening training run.

I had traveled to Baton Rouge for a *Wait Wait* show at the downtown performing arts center, one of about a dozen such trips I made each year, and as is often the case, I got an invitation to join some locals for a run. This time, though, the invitation came from Michelle Forte LeBlanc, owner of Fleet Feet Sports Baton Rouge, who asked me if I'd stop by the School for the Visually Impaired and talk to her running team. I had expected, when I came by toward dusk on this Wednesday evening, to meet a team of para-athletes who presumably traveled about the South and the country competing against other such athletes, and given that my own high school competitive career was not garlanded with laurels, I wasn't sure I would have anything to offer them.

I was, as I often am, wrong in every particular. There was no organized team here, no uniforms. Most of the kids in front of me were young, preadolescent. Some of them didn't even have sneakers. Bobby Simpson, the school's director — and a former mayor of Baton Rouge — was here to run with us, and he told me there were about seventy kids studying at the school, about fifty of them in residence, sent from all over the state, ranging in age from toddlers up to kids who could legally drink, if they could find a way to a bar. From the look of the drab 1970s institutional buildings, the school didn't have much money, and thus probably few extracurricular activities, and no sports to speak of. Looking up from the picnic table where I tried to field the kids' questions, you could see the towering modern, multimillion-dollar Louisiana State University football stadium, an amusing irony lost on the many present who couldn't in fact see it.

LeBlanc's notion was that kids needed exercise and purpose and a goal, so she had given them one. She organized the first-ever Louisiana School for the Visually Impaired No Boundaries 5K, to be held on the campus in early October, to raise awareness of the school and its students, and these were the nineteen kids who were going to run it. Tonight we were going to do two training laps around the campus, for a total run of about two miles. "Are you all ready to run?" asked Michelle, once I had run out of answers to the kids' infinite questions, and we all headed toward the driveway.

Luke, the kid who insisted that my friend William must have just known, somehow, about the bombs — because "he JUST DID" — immediately grabbed my hand. It was a little sudden, seeing as I had known him for all of seven minutes, but as had been explained to me, these kids live far from their families — assuming they have families. They can't go anywhere on their own, and nobody comes to take them away, so I was the most exciting thing to happen to them all week. Maybe all month. Maybe since they got there.

"Okay, let's go!" said one of the volunteers, and Luke shouted, "AAAAAAAAH!" and sprinted full out for twenty yards before he gasped and pleaded for a break. I kept encouraging him to pace himself, but moderation wasn't in him. He was a switch with two settings, walking and AAAAAAAAAH! After guiding the way halfway around the campus and talking about many things with Luke, I decided to run ahead and spend some time with another group. As I jogged away, he shouted, "HEY! You're not going to leave your kid behind, are you?"

Thanks, Luke.

Up ahead, two more volunteers were keeping a boy named Evan-Anthony company, if they could catch him. Evan-Anthony was by far the fastest runner of the bunch, although like Luke, he wasn't very good at moderating his pace. Evan-Anthony liked to stop, get down in a sprinter's starting stance, paw at the ground with one hand, growl like a tiger, and then take off. Evan-Anthony was five years old and had thick Coke-bottle glasses, through which he, too, seemed very happy to see me. Evan-Anthony's world, like that of all five-year-olds, was very immediate and very concrete — that bush, that tree, that building — all of which he sped toward, growling and happy.

I managed to keep up with Evan-Anthony as we finished the second circuit of the campus, and then I decided to circle back, running the way I had come, finding a new group of runners and guides, and then running them to the finish before starting back again. Each time I jogged back alone through the darkening evening, I thought — as has been my habit of late — about my own troubles and woes, and then twenty or fifty or a hundred yards later I would fall in with a child who had a much more serious problem, and a much better attitude about it.

Here was Brandi, eight, who wanted to be a cheerleader some day, which would require, among other things, that she be able to leave this school and find one with an athletic program, a school that could accommodate her disability. She was here, running along with me, because no such school was available to her. And then Luke again, who either couldn't see me in the dimming light or pretended not to, angry that I (too?) had abandoned him.

And then finally, the last runner of the pack, Lydia,* one of the few kids who was obviously, and completely, blind. She was walking carefully with her guide, who I volunteered to replace for this last half lap. Her eyes were sunken back in her head, only the whites showing. She was no bigger than an eleven- or twelve-year-old, but after a few minutes of conversation, it became apparent that she was older, much older — in fact, she was eighteen. She was very happy I had joined her, as she wanted to interview me for her current events project, and as we walked around the circumference of her world, her arm firmly holding my elbow,

*Not her real name.

194

she asked me about running: when I started, why I did it, and what I got out of it.

It's impossible if you talk about running not to eventually extol it as a cure for what ails you — your sedentary lifestyle, your twenty extra pounds, your depression, your anxieties — and as I walked along with Lydia, chatting about how through running I had managed to lose weight and gain energy, how I rarely caught colds, it occurred to me that my trials and my successes were all pissant little annoyances compared to what she endured as she woke every day to darkness.

I grew self-conscious and eventually asked her to tell me about herself. She has been blind since birth, she said, born four months premature. "Oh," I said brightly, "you must have been really eager to get here!"

"No," said Lydia, in a tone of patient correction. "I was a crack baby."

We were about fifty feet from the finish, which was delineated by all the other students and volunteers who had walked, run, or, in Evan-Anthony's case, growled around the campus two times and were now waiting for Lydia and me, the last two stragglers. I said to her, "Do you want to run?"

"How far is it?" she asked.

"Not far," I said.

She grabbed my arm tighter, and I said, "Go!" And I and Lydia — old and young, thick and thin, sighted and blind, ran for the finish.

The race went off as scheduled two weeks later, with the students and their guides running the five kilometers around the school under stormy skies and each getting a medal. The Delta Gamma sorority at LSU, which volunteers at the school, came to cheer the kids as they ran. I hope Brandi, my young friend who aspired to be a cheerleader, heard them. I hope she joins them someday. I hope she ends up on top of a pyramid of cheerleaders, because from such a height, you can see everything.

EIGHT

Like so much in life, filling a thousand cups with Gatorade is a matter of timing. Once you've got the cups arrayed in a tight rectangular matrix on the folding table, you need to fill each of them, not too much, which would make the cup too heavy and unstable to hand to a runner, and too difficult for her to swallow on the move without choking; and of course not too little, which would make the exchange of cup from volunteer to runner pointless, unless you think handing an exhausted, dehydrated person a near-empty cup is an amusing prank. As a rookie, you start by eyeballing the imaginary fill line, about a third up the side of the cup, but that becomes too cumbersome and eye-straining, so instead you start counting out the pour to time, one-two-three-four, one-two-three-four, before tipping up the pitcher and moving on to the next cup. Once you've got the hang of it, you skip the up and down, and just keep the pour going across the contact point between one cup's rim and the next (which geometry tells us is a single infinitesimal point, although we must allow for the fact that cheap paper cups are not platonic circles), with a brief stop before moving on. As Norman Maclean said of fly-fishing, "It is an art performed on a four-count rhythm," and as Norman Maclean also said, "All good things come by grace, and grace comes by art, and art does not come easy."

I finished the last of the cups lined up across the width and breadth of the table. The high school girls I was working with on this table grabbed two thin cardboard sheets and placed them carefully over the filled cups, and we started to stack more cups for a second story. It was six in the morning, and we had hours, and many cups, to go.

I found myself here, early on a cool October Sunday morning in 2013 at the mile-18 rest stop of the Chicago Marathon, stacking and filling cups because of a little error I had made two years prior, almost to the day, back in the halcyon days when I did not volunteer at marathons, I just ran them, and I was a married man with three daughters whom I still read to at night. I woke up on the morning of October 9, 2011

— my last morning as a decent human being — with what seemed a nifty notion. In a month I would be running the Philadelphia Marathon, and my training for this day called for a twenty-mile run at a brisk 7:30 pace. It just so happened that not far from my suburban home the Chicago Marathon would soon go off. Why not, I asked myself, jump on the course, run twenty miles with crowds and company, and step off the course right before the finish?

In running circles, a runner in an official race who has not paid the entrance fee or otherwise acquired an official bib or entrant number is known as a "bandit," and the act of doing so is called "banditing." To the forgiving, it is seen sometimes as a crime of convenience, as in "I didn't have time/money to enter, so I just bandited it," and sometimes even as an act of youthful rebellion, like jumping a subway turnstile or shoplifting from Neiman Marcus. For many years, there was a small subculture of runners who bandited the Boston Marathon each spring, starting about an hour after the official entrants had vanished down the road heading east from Hopkinton. They were tolerated in the same way that, in my youth, fans were allowed to run onto the field after a baseball team won a championship — as a kind of youthful exuberance, we'll allow it, but make sure nobody gets hurt, okay?

Pretty much every runner has bandited a race once or twice, for a mile or eight. They'll join a friend on the course for the last mile or the first; in fact, one of the runners at the finish line when the bomb went off in Boston in 2013 was shielded from injury by a relative who had jumped in to run with her to the finish; he took the shrapnel that would have hit her and the disabled daughter she was pushing in a wheelchair. My spontaneous notion to do it myself, on that October morning, was inspired by a friend who had paced someone for the last ten miles at the 2010 Chicago Marathon the year before, with no apparent ill effect to himself or the 45,000 registered runners including, that year, myself. In fact, in the six years prior to my own turn to the dark side, I'd run upward of fifty races, and each time I'd been a registered, honest runner with a bib. And in those races, the few bandits I knew about, and the many more I didn't, caused me no concern. As of October 9, 2011, I was a banditing virgin, and like all virgins, I approached my first time with some excitement, a little apprehension, and no real appreciation of the complications that might ensue.

My plan went off without a hitch. I took the train to LaSalle Street and North Avenue, near the five-mile marker. I waited for the three-hour pace group to zip by, then jumped in, a bottle of Gatorade strapped to my hand and energy chews in my pocket. My plan to take or leave nothing didn't quite work out: as the temperatures edged up into the seventies, I refilled my bottle twice from aid stations, and I did use one toilet along the route. Otherwise I bothered no one, as far as I could tell, and no one bothered me. I ran past the mile-17 aid station, waved to some of my friends who work it every year — they were surprised to see me — and arrived at mile 25, feeling pretty good about myself and my twenty-mile run. I slowed to a walk and headed to the side of the street where a policewoman raised the barrier tape for me to leave the course. I nodded in thanks. I believe she smiled. I strolled over to the Roosevelt Road L stop and hopped on the train home. If it was a crime, it was a perfect one.

Or, it would have been if I hadn't blabbed.

For two months, I had been keeping a training diary on the *Runner's World* website, in preparation for my attempt at a PR in Philly, and in the post I wrote later that day I didn't think twice, or even once, about mentioning my twenty-miler as an unregistered Chicago Marathon runner. Reading the entry now, I wince at the feigned breeziness of my guilty conscience. I even smirkingly offered to send Bank of America (the principal marathon sponsor) a check for the Gatorade I drank, if anybody were to complain. I must have known, somehow, that I wouldn't get away with it; the irony, of course, is that until I bragged about it, I had.

It was sometime the next day, Monday, when I first heard that comments were piling up on the blog post. And they were not praise for my admirably consistent pace in the twenty-miler. No, by the time the last of sixty-two comments had been posted, I'd been called a thief, a self-absorbed jerk, a loser, an idiot, an embarrassment to both my employer, NPR, and *Runner's World*, and most cuttingly, a "minor celebrity." I was scolded, threatened with violence — "Someone should smash him to the ground!" — and roundly condemned. One commenter laid out the case that banditing was the running equivalent of rape.

I had no idea that so many people thought of banditing a race as among the most mortal of sins, something that would place you in the deepest levels of Dante's hell. My crime brought out the most indignant moralizing it has ever been my shame to receive, including a painstakingly handwritten letter from a mom who told me that my actions had completely contradicted her years-long quest to teach her sons to be thoughtful, honest, and good. I was the murderer of even the possibility of virtue in a fallen world.

After about a week, the flood of judgment subsided, the emails, blog comments, and handwritten letters stained with bitter tears stopped arriving, and I started looking forward to returning to obscurity. I hoped for the day when somebody might steal a paraplegic's racing wheelchair and take my place as running's most hated man. Then a *Wall Street Journal* reporter came across the blog, and the story of my immortal, immoral run ran on its front page — and the condemnations poured in anew.

I had to admit, even as I grumbled about the unfairness of it all, that I had done wrong. But how wrong? Who had I harmed, how much had I harmed them, and what, if anything, should I do about it? So, as an exercise in abnegation, I decided to find out.

The first person I consulted was a rabbi, learned in Talmudic ethics. I laid out the story to Rabbi Douglas Sagal of Westfield, New Jersey, who stroked his beard, cocked an eyebrow, and considered. As he is my brother (and you know how brothers are), he stunned me by saying, "I don't think you did anything wrong."

"There's a principle in the Talmud called Ganeyv-Daat, which means to mislead," he said, sounding quite sage. "But you didn't do that. There was no intent to deceive. It wasn't Rosie Ruiz.* You didn't tell people you were planning to enter the marathon, run part of it, and claim you ran the whole thing officially. Your actions didn't cause anybody to suffer a loss. You didn't take anyone's place, so I would argue there's no ethical transgression."

Reassuring! Yet I couldn't take it as definitive. I sought a second opinion, from Chris-

*The woman who "won" the 1980 Boston Marathon by taking the subway to a spot a half mile short of the finish line and then running across it, three minutes before the first actual female finisher, Jacqueline Gareau. Ruiz was actually crowned the winner — literally, with a laurel crown, as they do in Boston — before witnesses came forward to expose the scam a week later, because in those more innocent days no one could imagine anyone doing that.

tine M. Korsgaard, Ph.D., a Harvard professor and a foremost expert on the moral philosophy of Immanuel Kant. Many of my critics made an argument that began with "What if everyone did what you did?" and in doing so, were unknowingly (perhaps!) relying on Kant's seminal 1785 *Groundwork of the Metaphysics of Morals.* Kant called this notion "the categorical imperative," and Professor Korsgaard proceeded to beat me about the head with it.

"It's applied as a thought experiment," she wrote to me. "Imagine a world in which everyone acts on the same principle that you do, and ask yourself whether, in that world, you could act that way, too." I understood this as a formal statement of the turnstile principle: If you jump a turnstile, the subway will run fine without your $2.25. If everybody jumped the turnstile, the subway would collapse for a lack of funds and nobody would go anywhere. And since you can't stop anyone else from jumping the turnstile, you have a responsibility to at least make sure you don't do it. The professor also took issue with my argument that I had used few public resources in my run: "Why does the public consent [to let the marathon use the roads]? Maybe the public just approves of marathons, and wants to support them. Or maybe the public gets something in return — the thrill of watching a race, caring who wins, etc. If that's how it goes, the fact that you didn't enter at the starting point or try to finish doesn't excuse you: it makes it worse. You were using just about everybody as a mere means to your ends. So that means you messed up pretty badly. I love your show."

Thank you, professor.

Finally, I called Carey Pinkowski, the longtime race director of the Chicago Marathon. If I had committed a crime, then Pinkowski had the best claim to be a victim — and was the one person who could, legitimately, sit in judgment.

"You don't have to pay for the Gatorade," Carey said, magnanimously. But, whether or not he knew it, he was a Kantian: he stressed that the risk to the race organizers was not one person drinking sugar water he didn't pay for, but an unknown number of people on the course cumulatively taking up space and resources with no ID, no way to know their medical history, and no way to track them.

"We forecast all our allotted resources, fluids, security, medical personnel, against a number of participants," he said. Each unregistered runner is an additional strain on resources, and each one on the course puts them one step closer to not being able to manage the event.

Now, he never would have said this to me — no race director would — but a marathon can handle a certain number of unregistered participants. If it couldn't, the whole thing would have fallen apart the second I stepped onto the pavement. A marathon is not as fragile as, say, the door that Jack and Rose tried to get on after the *Titanic* sank, which flipped over if one too many people tried to take advantage. But above a certain, unknowable number — A hundred bandits? A thousand? — the event becomes increasingly unmanageable. Thus, the Chicago Marathon officially has a zero tolerance policy for bandits, even the official entrant's friends who jump in to pace a runner in the last mile, let alone the entitled mooks who run a whole twenty.

When I asked Carey what penance I could perform, he offered two choices. I could work a shift at the chip verification station at the expo for an upcoming Chicago Marathon, sitting there for hours, making sure runners had the right packet, so as to understand how thorough the marathon is about making sure every participant is correctly accounted for. Or, I could take a shift at a water stop — "The last shift, when everybody's been through it," said Carey, cheerfully — with a broom and a bucket, cleaning up thousands of cups, so I could observe, firsthand, how much work and supplies and drudgery goes into looking after the paid, official, honest runners.

And that's how I ended up at the mile-18 aid station two years later (I was out of town for the 2012 Chicago Marathon) filling and stacking layers of Gatorade cups along with some high school girls. And I was glad to be there, and grateful for the chance to make amends.

I don't think banditing is equivalent to theft or, please, rape; I still don't know who the victim is of a single act like mine. But if there is any true value in running as a sport, it is that it is a great leveler. Runners don't gear up, armoring ourselves like football players; we strip down to the minimum and empty our hands and become what we are at our most natural, and thus we are reduced to what we all have in common: legs, lungs, heart, and mind. We are all out there on the same course, heading the same way, whatever our speed, a brother/sisterhood of chafed thighs and aching feet. My offense wasn't so much against the race organizers or the other runners — neither of whom knew I was there — but against the notion of this fellowship. Even though I thought I was joining all the registered runners on the course that day, what I was in fact doing was separating myself from them, and using them, as Professor Korsgaard said, for my own ends.

As a runner, you spend a lot of time by yourself, during all those miles, thinking of yourself as independent; it is your pace, your legs, your heart, your fatigue, your strength. It's easy to think of yourself as being solitary and alone, doing what you must and devil take the hindmost. But at a certain point — when you join a running group or start recognizing people in your circuit of local races or just start looking around you as you pass the same streets over and over — you realize that you're trying to break out of that shell and create a community around yourself. And if that's what you want, to run with people, to have people to run with, then you've got to treat them with respect. You wave when you see people out at 6 AM on a frozen morning. You never, ever respond to someone else's race result, no matter how slow, with anything but thrilled congratulations. And you don't bandit races. Because, as Kant tells us, if everybody did it, we'd all be back to running on our own, and there wouldn't be an "everybody" to run a race with. But also, as I discovered, because it is a way of separating yourself from the crowd, by letting them know you're better or smarter or more clever than the dumbasses who paid. And, of course, the thousands of suckers who got up early and put on their volunteer caps and worked for six hours or more to make the whole thing happen.

The stacking and filling was done. The girls and I had built a remarkable thing, a trembling sculpture of paper and liquid, painstakingly created so as to be picked apart hours later, a sugar-water version of a Tibetan mandala. Looking at it, I felt a profound sense of satisfaction, as great — maybe greater — than I had finishing my first marathon. That had been my own achievement, done for myself, and by myself — without a thought (I had spared none at the time) to the thousands of people who had cleared the roads and put up the signs and poured out the Gatorade and water and patrolled the race before, alongside, and after me. But this morning's work, although not something I could brag about, or be congratulated for if I did, was done purely in service. As we admired our creation, the people who we would serve were arrayed in a long snakelike progression, racing or running or struggling at a walk, and when they arrived I would be in a position to give them a little help. We were ready. We were willing. We were happy.

I picked up a cup of Gatorade from the top row, right at the edge, drank it — volunteering is thirsty work — and awaited the opportunity to serve. The first cohort of runners was some miles away but getting closer. I thought about the time two years before, when I had been among them.

NINE

The problem with being a midlife-crisis runner is that once you start, you're already in decline.

I had run my first marathon in 2005 at the age of forty, coming in at 4:03, and then learned to train more wisely and effectively, and managed to cut more than forty minutes off my time to run a 3:20 the next year. It was an impressive achievement that got me into Boston for the first time, and I was duly impressed with myself.

But in the years afterward, even as I kept up my regular training and ran one or two marathons every year, despite my effort or intensity of training my finishing times increased by a few minutes each time. I ran Boston in 2011 under sunny skies and a cool following wind, and even with excellent preparation I still finished in 3:27, seven minutes slower than my best marathon time five years prior, and felt like I had nearly killed myself to do that. Was that it? Was I done? Were my best days in fact behind me?

According to Professor Ray Fair of Yale University, yes, they were. An economist, Fair had run statistical analyses for race results of thousands of elite runners over many years and determined that, on average, marathon times inevitably decline about a minute per race for every year of age past forty . . . no matter what. So, as I hobbled away from the finish line in Copley Square, I wondered: should I just resign myself to increasing finish times and body measurements, and enjoy my slow journey downward on Professor Fair's slope, until the reverse roller coaster dropped me into the abyss at age sixty?

Or . . .

Would it be possible, at (what then seemed to me) the impossibly old age of forty-six, to run my best marathon ever? I had no idea what such a thing would require. I had already logged a lot of miles, and by finishing a marathon in under 3:30, I'd proved I was in the top percentile of amateur athletes my age. What would it require to reverse the arrow of time, if only for a year?

In the end, it required a lot, and most of what it required was miles — but not, by any means, all of it. In the end, making the attempt at my PR, which I decided to do at the Philadelphia Marathon on November 20, 2011, required me to change everything I thought about running, and racing, and what constitutes success.

There are not a lot of training tips in this book, because in general I am skeptical that training advice is useful for most runners. It's analogous to writing advice. You want to be a writer? Don't worry about the brand of pen or paper or software or exercises or outlines, just sit down and write at whatever time of day and in whatever room works for you. The more you write, the better a writer you will become. You want to be a runner? Run when you can and where you can. Increase your mileage gradually, as I laid out in an earlier chapter, and your body will respond and you'll find yourself running farther and faster than you ever thought possible. "Just do it," to quote a company whose name I can't quite remember right now.

And yet, in this, I'm a hypocrite. My first marathon, Chicago 2005, was run after I made almost every training mistake I could make. I ran too far and too fast too early and injured myself, I didn't eat well, and I didn't include enough long slow distance runs (partly because of the injury), and although I finished the race in 4:03, I suffered mightily and unnecessarily. For the following year's race, I corrected my ways: I joined the same running group I run with to this day, and I went from running six or even seven days a week to running just three.

That training plan, called Run Less, Run Faster and created at the Furman Institute of Running and Scientific Training (FIRST) at Furman University, applies an essential insight to running: too much of anything is bad. When I ran every day, ramping up my mileage every week, I put a strain on my body and something snapped (as it turned out, it was my piriformis nerve). By running every other day, you allow the body to heal, and by cross training on off days — biking, swimming, or any other cardio — you maintain fitness while avoiding burnout. The three training days were hard — track work on one day; fast, mid-distance tempo runs on the second; long, slow distance on the third — but the cumulative effect was impressive, and the lower weekly mileage and rest days helped make sure I didn't injure myself (again). The result: I cut forty minutes off my marathon time, and ran a 3:20:41, setting my PR and qualifying for the Boston Marathon for the first time by nineteen seconds.

But in the five years that followed, as I continued to train using the Furman method with my friends who were doing the same, I fell into Professor Fair's rut: I was doing the same thing at the same intensity but losing speed as I aged. To go faster — to go much faster, cutting more than seven minutes off my April time by the time November rolled around — I would have to run more. Much more. I consulted the experts at *Runner's World,* including former Boston champion Amby Burfoot, and they created for me an exact and demanding training schedule.

It was daunting. My usual marathon training had me running thirty miles a week, perhaps thirty-five or forty on those weeks with a twenty-mile run on the weekend. This schedule would double it, to sixty miles a week and beyond. I would do the runs on a strict schedule, changing from hill work in the beginning, to build a base of leg strength, to speed work and tempo runs, along with long runs. One day on the schedule, about twelve weeks into the sixteen-week training period, called for a ten-mile tempo run on a Saturday, followed by twenty miles the very next day. Good news: I could slow down for the twenty miles. Thanks, Amby!

My training did not begin auspiciously. It was my own idea to inaugurate my attempt on my own record with a half marathon, a serendipitous race I was able to fit in while on a family trip to visit my then in-laws at their home in a small town in Minnesota. As I walked up to the starting line, I actually thought of myself as a Big City Runner, come to teach these country folk a thing or two about half marathonin'. Sure, it was 80 degrees out, but I figured I'd smoke my age group, then, perhaps, in my generous way, hang out by the finishers' chute and cheer on the local hoi polloi.

Instead, one hour and thirty-eight minutes later, I was flat on my back on the grass, trying to suck in that soul-moistening humid air of a hot Minnesota summer, thinking that giving in to death might be simpler. The idea of running twice that distance at the same pace — which I'd have to do to beat my PR — seemed less likely than spontaneously evolving wings and flying it. As I gasped for air, it occurred to me that I was beginning my quest to stop growing older exactly how I had started growing older in a New Jersey hospital room forty-six years before: lying prone, trying to figure

217

out how to breathe.

The actual schedule began with four miles of running hills, to build leg strength and prevent further injury down the line. That wasn't a problem, but the utter lack of hills in the glacier-polished plains west of Chicago was. Instructions were instructions, however, so my quest to turn back the implacable march of time began with me running up, and over, and up, and over an overpass crossing the I-290 expressway. I hummed the *Rocky* theme to myself, but I could not hear it for the traffic noise.

The schedule then called for a slow, gentle progression for the first few weeks, adding just a single extra day of running at first, for four days a week. The tough part, at first, wasn't so much fatigue as getting used to a new daily (or near daily) rhythm. I had always filled in my off-running days with another workout — a swim or a bike during my flirtation with triathlons, or a trip to the gym or a yoga class. Now, there were no nonrunning days. Instead of trying to put on the right gear in the dark — Spandex? Flippers? Both? — I just got up, put on shorts and shoes, checked the assigned mileage, and stumbled straight out the door.

I had thought of myself as being fit, but my muscles missed their days off and let me know. One morning during those first few weeks I did eight fast miles on trails on a Tuesday, then got up on Wednesday to run more as instructed, and my lower legs, groaning and creaking like wooden beams in an earthquake, simply would not cooperate. Instead of running, I sat on a park bench and negotiated with my calves. "Come on, guys," I said. "I know this is tough, but it's got to be a team effort. The lungs are committed — right, guys?" My lungs coughed assent, and we agreed that all of my body parts would reconvene the next morning and see if we could get on the same page.

By the end of August, though, a remarkable thing happened. The aches began to fade, and then disappeared. I started to look forward to each day's run, because each day's run was getting easier. My running style, under the evolutionary pressure of daily runs, began to adapt. Instead of lowering my head and churning my legs to press through the end of a day's run, I tried to relax, stay upright, and tread lightly on the pavement. I imagined my midfoot gently landing on the ground, lifting off, alighting again. Through miles of feedback and constant revision — unclenching my hands, lowering my shoulders, activating my calves and ankles — I started to change my running style to something that could last. It wasn't beautiful, but nothing hurt.

About halfway through the four-month training schedule, it was time to measure my progress. On September 11, I joined the *Runner's World* editorial staff at the Chicago Half Marathon. I was feeling good, even cocky. In fact, I announced a bet: "If I beat every other *RW* staffer and contributor, then I get to pick the cover model for an upcoming issue." (I said this while pointing at myself and clearing my throat.) One of the editors, the fastest runner on the assembled staff, took me aside and said, "I've got to beat you, because if you're on the cover, sales are certain to tank."

I have always hated this particular half marathon. Most of the course is out on the concrete surface of Lake Shore Drive, which turns into a rock-hard frying pan on hot, late summer days, and my memories of it mostly involve trying not to give in to cardiac arrest as I staggered into the shade of the trees around the finish line. My PR for the course was a painful 1:29:23, a number written in blood and bile, and my goal for this race was simply to not give in to the perennial urge to kill myself on race day. I had always believed that if you had anything left in your tank when you crossed a finish line, you were doing something wrong. If so, then today — applying a lesson I had learned at the prior year's Chicago Marathon, which I had run so soon after breaking bones in my back — I was going to do it wrong intentionally.

The editor and I went out together at a smooth 6:50-per-mile pace and kept it up, and even as the temperature rose, I kept my cool. He pulled away around mile 6, but I didn't care — why, I was hardly racing! Just out for a quick stroll with a few thousand strangers on a sunny day in the traffic lanes of Lake Shore Drive! At any minute all of us might just decide to stop for a picnic. My pace was consistently sub-7 minutes per mile, and yet at the same time I felt completely within myself. I admired the trees and the grass and the concrete and kept running, and loped in at 1:29:15, two minutes behind Brian, and fifteen seconds better than my course PR. I had given up a chance to go after my half-marathon PR (1:28) and a chance to be on the cover of the magazine — I was even going to shave my chest — but I had gained something else: proof that success in racing did not have to equal misery.

This was a revolution. My personal highlight film of major race days is a catalog of self-inflicted miseries, like one of those "Faces of Death" videos from the 80s, and if you had asked me why I endured such tribulations in what is ostensibly my hobby, I would have said . . . Well, that's the point, isn't it? To see how much you can endure?

The project had begun with the assumption that in order to run faster as I got older I would have to suffer even more, following a graph line of rising pain proportionate to speed. But, it finally occurred to me, maybe success in running can be delinked from the amount of punishment you're willing to endure to achieve it. Maybe the point isn't to see how much you can stand, but to see what you can train your body and mind to do with less and less agita. Maybe the goal, as one ages as a runner and as a person, is not to learn how to suffer better, but to find your way toward a sense of ease and even — Had I ever used this word in the context of racing before? — pleasure. Is it possible, in this fallen world, to run fast and enjoy it?

When a month later the dreaded day came, that thirty-mile double-long-run weekend, I leaned into it. The ten-mile tempo run flew by, or rather I did, loping through my suburb at a ridiculous seven-minute pace, although as of that day it no longer seemed ridiculous. And the next morning, twenty miles at a 7:30 pace along the Chicago Marathon course during the race didn't seem hard at all. The last test before my marathon would be my neighborhood's 10K race.

As I have described, my midlife running boom was inspired in part back in 2003 when I watched that 10K race go right by the house I had just moved into. I ran that race the next year, and every year after it, my time coming down from forty-five minutes or so by thirty seconds each year, but never getting closer than six seconds to that seemingly impenetrable forty-minute barrier. If I was ever going to do it, this was the year, on a cool weekend just six weeks before the Philadelphia Marathon, ten weeks into the most rigorous training schedule I had ever endured, and while I was in the best shape of my life.

I started the race fast, as I had been starting every run, fast enough to PR, but it would take effort. Since I had abandoned punishing myself to get faster, I used geekery. In the rebooted 2004 version of *Battlestar Galactica,* when they want to move the bulky spaceship a vast distance very quickly, the crew "spins up" the "Faster-Than-Light Drive." Not "crank," not even the Star

Trekian "engage," but "spin up," a phrase that evokes effortlessly increasing momentum. So after clocking 6:18s or better for the first five miles, I started saying to myself, aloud, "Spin up! Spin up!" And so for the first time I think ever, I actually accelerated in the final mile of the race. I came roaring around the corner where I live, passed my house, waved without slowing down, and flew the final half mile to the finish, at light speed or better, crossing as the clock ticked over 39:09. My fastest time ever, by almost a minute.

At forty-six, I had just traveled through time and shown up as my seventeen-year-old self. I was trained, fit, and equipped with Faster-Than-Light engines, deployable at will. I was ready for the marathon. The only sour note: my daughters hadn't been there to cheer as I went by. They were still inside the house. I got there too quickly, too focused on the goal ahead.

Two days before the Philadelphia Marathon, I realized I had no notion of what the course would be like, other than that it would be about twenty-six miles long. So I consulted Ian Chillag, a *Wait Wait* producer, onetime Philadelphia resident, and 2:39 marathoner.

I asked him, "Any advice on the marathon?"

Chillag said, "Yeah, don't be stupid."

"Don't be stupid?"

"Yeah. You're always stupid. You always go out too fast. So don't be stupid. You want to negative split this course. If you cross that halfway mark faster than 1:37:30, I'll hit you."

I promised Chillag that if I arrived at the halfway point before 1:37:30, I'd stop and wait for the clock to tick over before going on.

As I went to bed at my Philadelphia hotel the night before the race, full of noodles and spicy pigs' ears from a hole-in-the-wall restaurant in Philly's Chinatown, I contemplated my secret — something I had told no one, not the *Runner's World* editors, not my running buddies, not Chillag. My stated purpose was to beat my PR, which meant sub-3:20. My informal, public goal was 3:15, which would give me a five-minute cushion in case something went wrong. But my secret goal, one which I dared not speak out loud for fear it could not bear the weight of the air, was to finish in under three hours and ten minutes, requiring running a touch under 7:15 per mile for a touch over 26 miles. I had run a 1:29 half with relative ease, and a sub-40 10K — why not a sub-3:10 marathon? Other than, that is, my advanced age and sparse natural gifts and the weight of my lifetime as a mediocre athlete? I tried to get some sleep, interrupted by fitful dreams of earless pigs mocking me for my presumption.

Every marathon begins with a kind of boast. The crowd behind the starting line is divided into "corrals," demarcated for runners at different intended paces, so as to prevent chaos in the first mile, as faster runners overtake or even trample slower ones in front. But even in those overpopulated races with strictly assigned corrals, such as the Boston Marathon, within those corrals people edge forward or retreat backward as an expression of their confidence at that moment, as derived from a complicated calculus involving weather, what they ate the night before, and anything else that might be twisting in their gut.

On this cool Sunday morning in Philadelphia, I had been assigned to the A corral, the first of three. At the very front of it were the elite runners — a smaller and less impressive group than might be seen at bigger, richer races, like Chicago or Boston — and then behind them, the rest of us: people who expected to run the race in about 3:15 or under. This was ambitious at my age and size and weight: forty-six years, 5'7", 175 pounds. But still, I edged forward, stepping around other runners until I could — mirabile visu — actually see the bony arms of the men who expected to win this thing. I wasn't expecting to challenge them, but I was imagining something perhaps just as unlikely.

On cool race mornings like this one, runners wear throwaway clothes to the starting line, to keep us warm until we are allowed to begin exerting ourselves. Some favor trash bags, with holes torn out for the arms, but I think this is an unnecessary attempt at economy, not to mention unflattering. Any runner — any person — has enough old clothes redolent of sweat or spotted with paint or still smelling like the person who abandoned it in your apartment when they moved out. In my case, I was wearing an old NPR shirt, produced for some long-ago marketing campaign. Although we hadn't started running, I wasn't feeling cold. Maybe anxiety produces heat. I took off the shirt and threw it into a bin provided so that discarded clothing could be distributed to the needy. I imagined a panhandler wearing the NPR logo, reminding passersby how much they relied on his panhandling and thanking them for their support.

This time, I wouldn't have to wait for the first wave to go off, or the second, before it was my turn. I was ready to jump at the first gun I heard. It fired, and I started to run. The field quickly spread, and I saw the elites lope away down Benjamin Franklin Parkway toward the towers of downtown at a sub-five-minute pace. For one brief moment, I enjoyed the once-in-a-lifetime experience of running "in the pack" behind the eventual winner of a marathon. Then they left me behind, and I concentrated on the race I had come here to run: the one against time. Running those first few miles, through downtown Philly to the Delaware River, I felt effortless confidence, like an adept of jiujitsu, a tea ceremony master, a poker player with nothing but aces. A friend took a photo of me in the early miles of the course, when I was reeling off seven-minute miles without any noticeable effort, and there I am: not only fit, with my extended left leg as Jim Fixx–like in its muscularity as it had ever been and ever will be, but also happy. I think about that day a lot now. I had always believed that suffering was a requirement for anything worthwhile: art, educational success, professional achievement, marriage, parenthood. On this day, I had found another way, though it had taken thousands of miles to get there.

Mile 5 flashed by, and we were back into downtown, with cheering crowds along Chestnut Street, and I felt great. I began to cultivate a feeling of holding back, like a bandage on top of an itch I really, really wanted to scratch. Another 7:05 mile. It was fast — it was very fast — but it felt easy. It even felt cautious — I wanted to run faster, and knew I could. For the first time in any marathon, I began looking forward to mile 20 . . . because it was then, and only then, I promised myself, that I'd let myself tear off the bandage and go.

Legs spun, thirteen miles passed, energy gels were ingested, and we returned to the Museum of Art. The half marathoners diverted off to their finish and we marathoners turned left to run around the building and head northeast on the parkway lining the Schuylkill River. If the first part of the marathon was a parade through Philadelphia's downtown core, the second half would be a trip out into the country . . . out and back on one road, six miles or so each way. The clock at the halfway mark read 1:33. I was way ahead of my stated goal pace, and two whole minutes under my secret one. I was being recklessly, intentionally stupid. Ian was going to hit me. "But first," I said to myself, "he's going to have to catch me."

By the time I hit the twenty-mile mark on an uphill stretch in the riverfront neighborhood of Manayunk, that "itch" had faded . . . the marathon had reasserted itself, as it will, but even if I couldn't accelerate through the finish as I had at the 10K, I was still two hours and twenty-four minutes into a marathon with six downhill miles to go, and anything was possible, including, it seemed, the impossible.

Then — tremors in my calves, those weird misfirings of nerves that feel like wires in your legs have been crossed, warning of cramps to come. It was calf cramps that cost me fifteen minutes in the 2009 NYC Marathon — I had watched my calf muscles spasm inward, leaving weird undulating half-inch indentations — and I wasn't going to let that happen to me again. I stopped dead, near the twenty-three-mile marker, and spent thirty precious seconds stretching out my calves. "Behave," I hissed at them. Would they listen? I started running again. I picked up speed. A mile flew by, no cramps. This was going to be amazing . . . a 3:05, maybe? Another mile zipped by, going downhill now. Gravity itself had signed on to Team Sagal! I got to the mile-25 marker and . . .

. . . BOOM. A gremlin whacked my hamstring with a ball-peen hammer: a sudden, vicious, explosive cramp. This had happened to me before, as well, in the 2006 Chicago Marathon, almost costing me my Boston qualifying time, and for a crazed moment I refused to believe it was happening again and kept trying to run on one leg, like Monty Python's Black Knight. I hobbled to the side of the road, stopping dead for the second time, and stretched out my leg on the fender of a car, pounding the muscle with angry fists, cursing it, pleading with it, while three whole minutes ticked away, and the 3:05 pace group streamed by me, puzzled to see a bald man arguing with his own leg by the side of the road. I was so close, in so many ways, to succeeding beyond my secret dreams. If I lost it now, a mile away from the start, and had to watch the clock tick past 3:20 as I walked the last mile, I don't think I could have borne it.

I pushed away from the car and ran a step. The leg ached, but the ache faded, and the cramp did not return. I absolutely refused to baby that leg, and insisted on accelerating back up to a seven-minute-per-mile pace: it was crazy, but at this point I was gambling with house money, and if my leg fell off, well, then dammit, I'd use it as a crutch to hobble the rest of the way. It seemed a miracle that this was possible: these steps, this mile, this whole race. I divided the last mile into quarters, and started bargaining with fate for each one. Just let me run this 400 meters, then you can tear my legs off. Okay, thanks, how about one more quarter mile? I came curving around the Museum, and the crowd all seemed to be shouting for me . . .

. . . I saw something strange to my left, a group of men kneeling on the pavement, as if in prayer, around something in the midst of them, which might have been a person . . .

. . . and then I was there, through the finish line, my watch reading 3:09. I had done it, definitively, smashing my PR of five years earlier by more than eleven minutes. I felt flush with achievement, with the energy, if not necessarily the legs, to run a victory lap around the whole damn twenty-six-mile course waving an American flag.

I had accomplished something that Dr. Fair's statistics had predicted would be highly unlikely, if not impossible. But I did not feel as if I had pulled off some kind of miracle on asphalt. I felt — I knew — that I had put in four long, difficult, painful, rewarding, exciting, revelatory months, my finest as a runner, transforming the impossible, mile by mile, into the possible. I had not reversed time, or gotten any younger. But I had shown, at least to myself, that time and age are not walls but fences, and fences can be jumped.

A number of people, including Chillag, suggested that next I set my sights on a sub-three-hour marathon, which among runners is the informal barrier between being an excellent amateur and simple objective excellence. Sub-three people, while not quite the separate species that sub-2:30 marathoners are, are still different from the rest of us. If you run a 3:09 marathon, you're a great amateur runner and you should be very proud, as I was. If you can run a 2:59 marathon, then you can do anything, including, perhaps, depending on the day and the field, winning the thing.

But no. I was exhausted and I knew that the gains from further training would decrease logarithmically. I had to essentially double my weekly mileage to get my 3:27 marathon time down to 3:09. Shaving off another ten minutes might require me to double the mileage again, and I was already pushing the limits of my family's tolerance, and perhaps my own.

Besides, the ambition wasn't there anymore. I had started the quest out of a deep-seated fear of my inevitable deterioration, and now that I had reversed its flow I was ready to relax and accept that now the tide would go back out. Beating back the ravages of time is a lot like trying to protect your sandcastle from the incoming tide, as I had done as a child and had done with my own children. You can delay but never prevent the inevitable destruction. I had proved something to myself, that I could accomplish something once inconceivable to me and, I would guess, to people who had known me either as the indolent brainy nerd I was as a child, or as the harried, slowly ballooning guy I had been in my thirties, as I was trying to juggle work and family. I was pleased, and I was proud, but I was also done.

As the marathon receded into the distance, I couldn't quite figure out what to do with myself. I kept running five or six days a week rather than three, but the intensity faded, and pretty soon, my Great Race was beaten ceaselessly back into the past. The next year, 2012, was the last year of my marriage, with its many and increasing trials, and during that time, and in the years since, I have often tried to hold on to that feeling from the early miles of the 2011 Philadelphia Marathon. Not the confidence, or even, God help me, the sense of having been well and truly prepared for what I was enduring, because I knew, as my divorce unfolded, that I had never trained a single moment for that. No: what I have tried to remember, and occasionally achieved, is that sense of handing myself over to the moment I was in, trusting that what had brought me there would carry me through, allowing things to transpire not with effort, but with something like ease, even grace.

TEN

When Erich Manser was thirteen, he was playing outfield for his youth baseball team in Ashburnham, Massachusetts. He had been an all-star shortstop but was moved back to center field after he started misplaying harder-hit grounders. Standing on the outfield grass, he heard the crack of the bat a hundred feet away. He looked up in the air and didn't see much of anything but light. A second later, he heard two distinct sounds: the ball thudding to the grass to his left, and to his right, more distant, a parent's voice saying, "I can't believe he *missed* it!"

It was around then, Erich told me, that he figured he'd better try basketball instead. Bigger ball.

Erich was born with retinitis pigmentosa, or RP, a genetic disease that causes the slow, irrevocable deterioration of the retina, leading, in most cases, to blindness by the age of forty. Erich was diagnosed earlier than most, at the age of five, when his parents realized that he couldn't see at all in dark rooms. "Night blindness" was in Erich's case the first symptom of RP, but as the disease progresses, the result is an implacable narrowing of the field of vision, from the periphery inward. By the time I met Erich three days before the 2014 Boston Marathon, he saw the world "as if through a cardboard toilet-paper tube." A small circle of blurry vision in front; nothing at all to the sides, above, or below.

Perhaps because it was a lifelong condition, and perhaps because its progression was so slow, but mainly because Erich is Erich, he never let his condition stop him from pursuing anything he wanted to do. Once baseball became impractical, he turned to basketball, starting as the center for his high school team (Erich is a pretty tall drink of water). But then the night blindness took over, and he found himself disoriented in the darker gyms. On a couple of occasions, he told me, he would be planted in the paint, waving for a pass, and then he would receive it right on the bridge of his nose. So, then, what came next? Swimming! A pool is brightly lit, the lanes are clearly marked, and all you really have to watch for is the big cross painted on the wall in front of you. Erich went toward swimming with the same energy he goes after anything, and even with just one year on the swim team — setting a high school record for the 50-meter freestyle that still stands — he managed to earn an athletic scholarship to Northeastern University.

(Let's pause here to remember that I quit my high school career as a competitive runner after one year, because it was too hard and I was tired of losing. And I can see.)

After college, Erich's journey to running was a lot like mine. He found a wife and a job and eventually there were kids, and like a lot of ex-athletes, he kept up his eating and drinking while dropping the training and found himself so overweight in his midthirties that even with perfect eyes he still wouldn't have been able to see over his belly to his feet. Members of his family had been runners, but he had always resisted; now it seemed like the simplest, most economical way to lose the weight and get back in shape. First a mile, then two, then joining a runners' group, then a first marathon, then another . . .

In April of 2014, at the age of forty-one, Erich had already run twelve marathons and a number of sprint and Olympic distance triathlons. In fact, it was his training for what would have been his first Ironman triathlon (2.4-mile swim, 112-mile bike ride, and a marathon) that tore his meniscus some months before, forcing him off his feet.* He had gained weight over the idle and indulgent holidays and started the New Year determined to get back on his feet and back in shape. He knew he couldn't run at the level he had once reached. But like everybody else in the running world, he wanted to be on the course for the first postbombing marathon. He contacted his friend Josh Warren and asked about getting on the team for Boston 2014.

"Have I got a guide for you," said Josh.

Like Erich and everyone else who had been anywhere near the Boston Marathon in 2013 — spectators, finishers, the thousands of runners who were prevented from finishing, and most bravely, some of the wounded — I swore immediately that I would return and run it again in 2014. Having gained some small amount of attention because of my proximity to the bombing, I was deter-

*Erich did his Ironman in 2015 — swimming and running tethered to a guide, riding the rear seat in a tandem bike — and finished in 11:10:28, setting the world record for disabled athletes in the event.

mined to leverage that publicity for the sequel. I came up with a plan to recruit an "All-Celebrity Team" of running guides who would compete to raise money for Team With A Vision in the 2014 marathon. I scanned the lists of celebrity marathoners, and imagined trading good-natured trash talk with the likes of Christy Turlington and Apolo Ohno in the months leading up to the race.*

But burdened by distractions and my own general lack of discipline, I wasn't able to pull it off. The only celebrity I successfully recruited was Drew Carey, who had in the prior years become a well-known runner, losing one hundred pounds and finishing the Marine Corps Marathon, his first, in a respectable 4:37. As a runner, Drew, who had been our guest a few times on *Wait Wait*, was delighted to be offered a chance to run Boston and signed up immediately, but he had to drop out a month before the race

*Allowing for a very loose definition of "celebrity," I am actually one of the faster celebrity marathoners. My 3:09 in Philadelphia in 2011 put me far ahead of the likes of Billy Baldwin (3:24) and Pamela Anderson (5:41). One of the few faster than me is Dana Carvey, of all people, who ran a 3:04 in 1972. Who knew?

with that most familiar of excuses: he'd been invited to compete on *Dancing with the Stars*. (Ironically, he was voted off the night before the marathon. Should have come with us, Drew!)

So in the end, I threw myself on Josh Warren's mercy. "Get me in this race," I said. "Find me somebody to guide."

Josh, unlike me, delivered. First, he was able to get me my own bib — usually a rare commodity, and almost impossible to come by this year — so I could run on my own as an official entrant. But I wanted to guide again, preferably for a veteran or someone else who had lost his sight to violence. As the Boston Marathon itself had become a battlefield in the ongoing grind of the "War on Terror," it seemed right and proper to honor somebody who had fought in it. But military veteran para-athletes have their own organizations, such as Achilles International's Freedom Team, so Josh had the next best thing: an athlete who was a hero in visually impaired running circles for his achievements on the roads and his advocacy for the blind, and — best of all! — because of an injury, he wasn't planning on running that fast.

On the Friday night before the Monday race, I met Erich Manser at a reception for

Team With A Vision at a mansion in Brookline, near the school the organization operates for visually impaired students. I was to speak to donors on behalf of the organization, and I was a little nervous about meeting Erich, who was delayed in getting there. Just like meeting William a year before, it felt like a first date that immediately became an arranged marriage. Mainly, I didn't want to disappoint him, either on meeting or during the race. Finally, he entered, a tall, bearish man wearing a visor and a grin, both of which rarely left his face in the time we spent together. Unlike William Greer, who didn't immediately register as a visually impaired person, Erich carried a white cane and had trouble finding my eyes with his as we greeted each other. We made small talk, and I introduced him to my parents and some friends who were there. "It's nice you were able to come for the whole weekend," he said.

"Yeah," I said. "Where else would I be?"

Marathon Monday I woke up (again) at my uncle and aunt's apartment in Brookline and walked through the dark streets at 5 AM to the school for the blind a mile away, where the bus would pick us up and take us to the race. Erich was not there — since he lived in a western suburb, it made more sense for him to go directly to Hopkinton. I climbed onto the bus with fifty other guides and runners, plus support staff, and we once again traced the route by bus that we would have to retrace on our feet. So far, so similar. But when we got to Hopkinton, everything was different. Security perimeters were set up at multiple points, each guarded by armed police. We went through so many checkpoints it seemed like we were starting a race in Baghdad. Even with all our clearances and permissions, we could get no closer than two blocks from the Vision Center, where the uniformed police forced us to stop our bus and walk. About twenty-five sighted people then slowly guided an equal number of blind people as we all gingerly worked our way down the sidewalk to the comforting, warm confines of the optometrist's office.

I was worried. In the winter of 2014, my running had become ragged. I had missed most of my runs with my group, catching up with them on weekends when I wasn't out of town. Most of my runs were on my own, and therefore slower, and usually shorter. I'm not sure and my records don't tell me if I even managed a single twenty-mile training run, usually essential to have any hope of success in a marathon. My running had become, really for the first time during my decade-long career as a middle-aged competitive amateur, a slog. I needed to do it, or I would become even more anxious than I already was, but my spark was dimming. The only thing keeping it aflame at all was that sense of vengeance — on the bombers, on the people who said the Boston Marathon would never be the same, and most of all on the inner voice that told me at random moments, late at night or first thing in the morning, that my grievous family losses were irretrievable. It seemed to me, without any evidence, that running the marathon again, guiding a blind runner again, crossing the line again, might restore the balance of the world to what it had been before. And that quest, that impossible dream, would have to be a workable substitute for actually, you know, training.

I had lined up to run the Boston Marathon the prior year just as the unraveling of my family had begun. I knew that what was to come in both cases would be painful, at times difficult, but I was still somehow confident that it would all turn out well. William Greer and I finished in Copley Square and were greeted by an explosion.

Then, a slower-moving conflagration engulfed and wrecked my family. In general, that infamous year had featured a lot of unpleasant surprises. So this time, on the morning of the 2014 race, I adjusted my expectations downward. Way, way downward. Bottomlessly so.

Erich wasn't at the Vision Center. He was delayed, somewhere, on his own way to Hopkinton. I got myself another cup of coffee, found a quiet corner, sat down, and thought about Chris Gleason.

> . . . I saw something strange to my left, a group of men kneeling on the pavement, as if in prayer, around something in the midst of them, which might have been a person . . .

Seconds later I was across the finish line, having set my triumphant 3:09 PR at the 2011 Philadelphia Marathon, and yet, throughout the next hour, amid the jubilation and bananas, I kept wondering about what I had seen. It was a person, I was sure of it, I could remember seeing his head . . . his head, yes, definitely a man, if only from the muscular arms and hairy legs. The torso had been blocked from my vision by the men kneeling around him. Men in uniforms.

Police? No, not dark blue, and they didn't have heavy equipment on their belts. Red-and-white uniforms. Red and white? EMTs? Yes. Most likely, EMTs.

At the *Runner's World* postrace party, as I happily gobbled up the cookies I had been denying myself for the past four months of training, people came up to me and asked me how I did, and I told them and they marveled and grinned and congratulated me, and I asked them if they knew anything about that one guy I saw lying on the ground near the finish, in some kind of medical trouble, and eventually somebody did: the rumor was that he had died. News reports flashing across our phones confirmed it: a runner had died, right near the finish line. Witnesses said he had collapsed to the ground just before the timer above the finish line turned over three hours, so I would have passed by a few minutes later, before he could have been moved. That was definitely the man I had seen on the ground. Later news reports gave his name: G. Chris Gleason, of upstate New York.*

*Chris was one of two runners who died that day on the course. The other was Jeffrey Lee, a twenty-one-year-old University of Pennsylvania student, who collapsed right after finishing the half-

My fleeting encounter with Chris haunted me for months after the race. I can still see him in his last moments of life, or more likely right after them, splayed on the ground, flat on his back, peaceful, as the seemingly reverent EMTs tried to save him. I googled his name every other day for weeks, hoping a news story would be posted, explaining the cause of his death. The internet never gave that up, but I learned a lot about him: he was forty years old on the day he died, a happily married father of two small children, a lawyer, and a force in the endurance sports community of upstate New York, known for his constant presence at races, training runs, triathlons, and the chat boards and websites devoted to that community. On the day of the Philadelphia Marathon, he was already a two-time Ironman finisher, with no known medical issues whatsoever, an amateur athlete in his prime. Hell, he was fit enough to run a sub-three-hour marathon, which he would have if he had survived another hundred yards. What stopped him?

The curiosity burned hard enough for long enough that I ended up contacting his

---

marathon. The cause of death, as with Chris Gleason's, remains unknown.

wife. Jennyfer Gleason, by then a widow for almost a year, demonstrated a grace in grief that I've thought about many times since and have tried (and mostly failed) to emulate. Part of it is her strong religious faith, which provides her and her children significant comfort. "It was just his time," she told me. "God said, 'Okay! I need you! This is it!' So he's up there, and getting everyone to run a little farther. 'Be better, stronger. Don't talk about it, do it!' " That explanation is at least as credible as any other, because the autopsy indicated . . . nothing. No toxicology, no hidden flaw in his heart, nothing. "His heart just turned into a bag of worms," said Jennyfer, quoting a doctor, who was as mystified as she was.

It's called "cardiomyopathy," which is a medical term for "We have no idea," and it happens, from time to time, to marathon runners, mostly male, mostly in the latter part of the race, and often right near the finish line. Some speculate that the burst of adrenaline or extra effort — just like the one I felt as I came around the curve to see the finish line, and then Chris, on the course in Philadelphia — is the tiny bit of extra stress that topples the function of the heart.

How often does this happen? A comprehensive study done by the Cardiology Division at Massachusetts General Hospital and Harvard Medical School, studying race data from 2000–2010, shows that of the 10.9 million runners who ran a marathon or half marathon in those years, fifty-nine experienced cardiac arrest, at a rate of about one runner per 200,000. And yet, even with solid numbers of how many die in the attempt, the study's authors concluded that "marathons and half marathons are associated with a low overall risk of cardiac disease and sudden death." Because, as it happens, you have a much higher risk of dying of cardiac arrest if you are obese, have high blood pressure or cholesterol, and/or are indolent . . . all of which are factors that can be alleviated or eliminated by — let me check, it's here somewhere, oh, yes here it is, what a surprise — running.

But marathoning remains special, and especially intimidating, because to run one goes far beyond what is merely required for good health or weight loss or an improved physique. To simply run makes excellent sense. To run a marathon is to go beyond sense, to risk something, maybe everything. The marathon has been associated with the risk of death ever since the event was invented by Phidippides, who came in first in a field of one and then promptly died.

Whether he existed (probably) or actually ran from Marathon to Athens to deliver news of military victory before promptly expiring from the strain (probably not), the marathon, based on his legend, was born with the notion of sudden death wrapped inside it. Mortality comes standard.

Here's something Winston Churchill actually did say, in his youth: "Nothing in life is so exhilarating as to be shot at without result." Such a truth implies that people seeking exhilaration will tend to put themselves in situations where they might in fact be shot at, literally or figuratively. And indeed even at my most physically and mentally exhausted, my teeth chattering and my mind blank from hypothermia (Boston 2007) or my legs rigid with cramps (New York City 2009) I was still, as I stumbled through the chute and clutched at my medal, thrilled. I had tempted fate. I had flirted with Phidippides. I had dangled myself as bait before the grim reaper, and scampered away before he could catch me. I had survived. So far.

What if today would be different? I was without question going to do something I was not adequately trained to do. I was under extraordinary stress, involved in a difficult divorce that was now in its second year and showed no sign of resolution. My journey from 2013 to 2014, from one Boston Marathon to another, had also seen me go through a complete transformation, a sudden detour into the nether regions. Dante had completed his own infernal journey by descending to its utmost depth and then piercing the border and passing through to purgatory and then heaven. Maybe I would follow. Maybe I should. So many times over the past year — on my motorcycle, on my couch — I had contemplated whether it would be better to end my particular divine comedy now before it got any worse. I had been a dramatist, once, and surviving the 2013 bombing to return to the 2014 race and then to run it all the way to the line where death would then return to claim me after my narrow escape the prior year — that was poetic, whether just or not. I could live with going out that way.

Enough, I thought to myself. Nobody was going to die today. The last thing Boston needed was more bodies.

I got up from the floor of the Vision Center's examination room. Erich still wasn't there. So I did a local TV interview without him, and had a bagel, and chatted with other runners and guides. There was Aaron Scheidies, one of the premiere blind runners in the country, who was looking to set the visually impaired marathon record that day; Jen Shelton, so fast she once famously outran her first guide, and arrived at the pickup point for the second guide sightless, alone, and shouting for directions. There was Ron Abramson, a wiry lawyer from New Hampshire, and Dan Streetman, a former Army Ranger, who had both, like me, volunteered to be marathon guides, and unlike me, looked like they were in shape to do it.

Erich finally arrived, delayed almost an hour as he tried to get through the security cordon around Hopkinton, but seemingly unperturbed by his travails, with his grin and visor intact. As I was to learn, much like William Greer, Erich never complains, about anything, despite his surfeit of reasons. Maybe I could absorb some lessons from him; after all, he also found it difficult to see his kids. (I was known around Team With A Vision for my tasteful sense of humor.)

We went over, again, how he liked to be guided. Unlike William, he had run with guides many times, and he had a preferred technique. He carried a tether with him, a three-foot length of bungee cord with loops at each end. I would carry one end, he the other, not so much for navigational guidance — even with the many changes to the marathon security measures since the prior year, it was still the same course, pretty much a straight line from Hopkinton to Boston — but for reassurance. He was perfectly capable of putting one foot in front of the other, and running in a more-or-less straight line, just like William. But in a massive crowd, the blind or visually impaired can feel disoriented. Add to this his night blindness, which meant that what registered to me as a shadow — from a tree, say, blocking the sun just for a moment — would be for him a complete and instant blackout. Perhaps this is less true for people blind since birth, but even with Erich's composure, confidence, and achievements, he still couldn't help reacting viscerally to the sudden onset of the dark, and the threat of the unseen. My job was to provide reassurance as much as guidance.

I could do that. I thought.

Talking to Erich, joshing with Josh, meeting the other runners and guides, each of them bouncy and jittery and raring to go, I found myself getting excited to run the race. I started to forget the events of the past year and remembered what had been a bass note under the dirge for my family: my determination to be here, on this day, and do this, as a gesture of defiance and resurrection. In an interview with the *Chicago Sun-Times* right after the bombing, I had said I'd like to send a message to the (then unknown) bombers: "Go fuck yourselves." (The *Sun-Times* didn't print it.) The two bombers were now respectively dead and in prison. But it was still a message worth sending, and this was still the best way to send it, en masse and in motion.

It was time to head to the starting line. We walked about into the sunshine. It was a beautiful day, cloudless and sunny, perfect for photographs but perhaps not so much for marathon running. Marathoners are like tuna salad: we go bad in the heat. The starting corrals were nuts. With the added mazes of fencing and security — our bibs were checked three times before we found our way to the actual roadway — we couldn't even get up to our assigned corral, and so we settled for the one behind it.

But that was a stroke of luck, as we found ourselves next to Dan and Ron and their assigned runner, Corvin Bazgan, a thirty-nine-year-old living with Usher syndrome, which is essentially retinitis pigmentosa combined with hearing loss. He had Erich's limited field of vision, and without his hearing aids (sweat wasn't good for them) he couldn't hear much, so I remember him seeming blissed out, above it all, grinning in the general direction of his two guides and us.

With all of us wearing our bright red Team With A Vision shirts, we felt, well, like a team, if one with variable levels of vision. It was 11 AM on April 21, 2014. There was a horn. We started to shuffle forward. I held tightly to the loop in the tether — Erich had doubled it, so as to keep me closer in the jostling crowd of the start. I looked up at him. His eyes darted around. He took in the scene around him in tiny sips, as if he were trying to drink a cocktail through the little plastic stirrer. He was grinning.

After a few moments of shuffling, I once again reached the starting line of the Boston Marathon. I had lived a year filled with catastrophes, only one of which was a bombing. But, for the next four hours or so, I would not be a father bereft, a tragic hero living out my own private opera. I would just be a guide. I would never finish the race if I dragged all that with me. So I dropped all of it on the pavement and ran.

The first seven miles flew by. Quickly realizing we could and should join forces, the five of us — three guides, two runners — formed a kind of flying wedge. Dan took the point, using his West Point–bred authority to quietly but firmly issue commands to runners in front of us to make way. I noted, enviously, that there was something about his tone that caused people to almost jump out of his way, without even a look back. I told him I wanted to hire him to precede me through life. He laughed without losing focus.

I had let go of the tether, as Erich felt comfortable running free in his protective cordon. We all felt great. We fed off one another's energy. We talked. Ron had also gone through a divorce and remarried. He expressed condolences for the death of my marriage. This time, I didn't go on about it. Why bring up anything sad on a day such as this, with such a group, in such a place? Ron and I took turns relaying cups of Gatorade from the aid stations back to the runners under our watch. We waved to the crowds. People cheered us on. We nodded to express that variety of gratitude that indicates complete agreement with the praise offered. All of us were smiling as much as Erich was. Heavy metal played from a speaker at a water station. "It's Dio!" said Erich. "I love Dio!"

"So," I said, "you're deaf, too?"

Everybody laughed, and we ran on.

Nothing good can last forever, and so it was with our impromptu group. Erich wanted to run at a faster pace than Corvin, so we said (and shouted) our farewells and everybody wished everybody else good luck. Erich unfolded his tether, which he'd been carrying in his hand, and put his fingers through the loop on one end. I held on to the other, and I led him on toward the halfway mark. The sun reached its peak at noon, blazing down on us. I cried out, "Blind runner coming through!" trying to emulate Dan's tone of unquestionable command. It was immediately questioned. "Could you, uh, not do that?" asked Erich, as gently as he could. "I just don't like taking advantage of my condition." He would have mentioned that to Dan, he said, but everybody was having so much fun with the Flying Wedge of Blindness that he didn't want to kill the mood.

Fair enough. I held on to the tether and kept going, trying to lead him clear of other runners. Whenever Erich got into a tight group of runners, he started to feel uneasy — again, understandable, if you imagine running surrounded by people you can hear but can't see. The same situational anxiety meant we ran well to the left and away from the shouting women of the Wellesley Scream Tunnel. I shrugged an apology at them: "Get you girls next time!" The sun continued to beat down. Erich fell silent, and so did I. This day was going to be a lot tougher than my run with William, for a number of reasons. Which is why I started to panic when the drugs began to kick in.

I wonder, sometimes, how and why none of the therapists I consulted over the years, from college to just before my marriage exploded, diagnosed me with depression. Perhaps my symptoms did not present as treatable via medication, even after the advent of Prozac. Perhaps I masked it by being clever and funny, which is how I had masked a lot of things. But in the fall of 2012, around the time I found myself having to wait until I stopped sobbing before leaving my car (a BMW 3 Series, the number one car for middle-aged men to sob in, alone) and entering the house, I realized I quite literally couldn't survive without medical intervention. I contacted one of the shrinks I had seen and more or less demanded chemical help. He was willing, and I ended up entering the growing population of the psychoactively medicated.

My medication — Cymbalta — was helpful. Very much so. There were many, many times during the year and a half since I had started taking it when I was dealing with some extraordinary interaction with my children or their mother, or some setback in the expanding legal fight, where I was able to both comprehend how bad things really were and yet stay on my feet, dealing with it, while knowing that my unmedicated self would have been driven to wailing, crumpled misery. I was often depressed or upset or sad or angry, but with good reason, and within reason. The world no longer presented itself to me only in varying shades of black. And because of that, I chose, every day, to remain in it.

That important benefit aside, I didn't like the side effects. I had gained weight and experienced an intermittent dizziness. The good news is that it only happened on rare occasions, and then only when I was engaged in intense physical exercise. Like, you know, running.

The sun was at its apogee and the heat

was starting to matter, but still, I shouldn't have felt this woozy, fuzzy, and dizzy. This was a common experience in the last year, something that had affected my training significantly. Worse, I had left my pill bottle in Chicago when I flew to Boston, so I might have been dealing with withdrawal, which seemed to manifest as an intense increase in the drug's side effects. I tried to focus. I ran. I wobbled, and straightened, and ran some more. If it had been just me, I would have stopped running and gotten off the course and sat down and had a cold drink and maybe a cigarette, who knows. This running thing was not working out, maybe time to try another vice.

"Hey, Erich!" cried someone to our right, looking back over his shoulder. It was a runner with a Team With A Vision bib that read GUIDE, but there was no blind runner to be seen around him. His name was Monte Harvill, and his guidee had "blown up," as we once said in more innocent times, just a few miles in, so once Monte delivered his runner to a medical tent, which would tend to him and transport him to the finish line, he continued running the race. Why not? It was the 2014 Boston Marathon. Who wouldn't want to run the whole thing?

I knew somebody. As soon as I saw Monte,

and he fell in with us, forming another, albeit smaller flying wedge for Erich, I realized I had been given an out. For the last mile or more, I'd been hanging on for Erich's sake, and now I was being released from that burden . . . maybe. There was an aid station coming up. I maneuvered around so I was running next to Monte and said, "Look, I'm having a real hard time. Do you think you could take over for me?"

"Sure," he said, seemingly glad to be occupied again.

I dropped back a step and ran next to Erich.

"Erich, I'm sorry, man, but this heat, or something, is getting to me. I have to stop for a while."

Erich told me later that he knew I was having trouble because I had stopped talking.

"Don't worry about it, man. If you have to stop, let's stop, it's fine."

"No!" I said. "Monte's got you. I'm sorry, but I'm just falling apart."

We said our goodbyes, and thanks and apologies, and I edged to the side of the road, stopped running, and walked up to the aid station. A volunteer handed me a cup of Gatorade. I thanked her, and stepped off the course to drink it, and to watch Erich

261

and Monte vanish down the road.

I stood there, my heart pounding, my head still spinning. I drained another cup of Gatorade. This was worse than death; this was failure. In the end, just as I had feared would happen when I guided William the year before, I had promised somebody I'd be there for him and I couldn't do it. I cheesed out. I hadn't been strong or dedicated enough. I'd blown it. Well, add the 2014 Boston Marathon to a long list of things attempted but not conquered: marriage, fatherhood, lawn maintenance, baseball . . .

I got another cup of Gatorade, and as the runners streamed by, I thought about Jacob Seilheimer.

I ran the 2007 Boston Marathon as a qualified, registered entrant, into the teeth of a freezing rainstorm, in about three hours and thirty minutes. I was forty-one, had trained hard and well, and was in the best shape of my life. Jacob Seilheimer was twenty-six years old, 6'2" and 360 pounds, and he had started out so far behind the last registered entrant he hardly counted as a bandit. His final time? Somewhere north of eight hours, he's not exactly sure.

I had never met Jacob, nor talked to him,

but I knew about him. While I was training for Boston 2007, somebody had pointed me to his website, "What Would Jacob Do?" Pictured there was this indolent obese man, who had decided to "run the Boston Marathon" on a whim, without adequate training, physical capacity, or, of course, qualifying or registering for the race. And reader: I hated him.

Not personally, of course, although my disapproval of everything about him took on an emotional heat. I had trained my guts out to qualify for Boston, and then again to run it decently, and this guy, who gave his weight as 450 pounds at the start of his training, just decides he's going to "run" the Boston Marathon by shuffling down the course long after the rest of us? Not only was it an affront to our — my! — achievement, it was a terrible idea. Anybody with any ounce of sense knows that deciding to go from "couch to marathon" is exactly the wrong way to start running. Decide to do something impossible! Make yourself miserable attempting it! Maybe die from a coronary! Good idea, pal.

I ran the 2007 race and flew back to Chicago and checked in on Jacob's website. There were pictures of him "running" the "Boston Marathon" by shuffling down a sidewalk in Framingham. Hah. And then, with a last smug sniff, I forgot about Jacob Seilheimer.

Except I didn't. I thought about him from time to time, usually as the Dumbest Runner I Had Ever Heard Of. I might have mentioned him in that capacity once or twice, over the years. Maybe it was just a lingering affront from his stealing our glory. Maybe it was a weird side effect of my fixation with weight — there, but for the grace of obsessive running, go I.

Years later, I decided to make some use of this odd but persistent memory and write about him for *Runner's World,* as an illustration of What Not to Do, the Goofus to my Gallant. But if I was going to do that, fairness required I actually talk to him. Thanks to Facebook, it was easy to find him in Andover, Massachusetts, where he works as a tax consultant, and thanks to NPR, he recognized my name and was happy to talk to me.

Jacob had always been a big guy, but also an athlete; he played football as a lineman at Colby College. But after his graduation, his father died, and he had to go to Texas to help dispose of his family's beekeeping business, and, well, "I was stressed, depressed, unsure, and was eating and drinking way too much . . . and by the time I went to law school in New Hampshire, I weighed 450 pounds."

He had some friends there who regularly joined the crowds of bandits who ran the Boston course after the official entrants every year — this of course was before the post-2013 crackdown — and in January 2007 one of those friends, Mike Moran, urged Jacob to do it with them. That very year. Three months later. "He was trying to find a way to help me to not be so fat," Jacob told me. "So he said, 'You can do it! You just have to get in decent shape!' And I said, okay, and then he put up a website and sent a press release to all our friends! So I figured I had to do it."

Driven almost entirely by a desire not to quit in front of his friends and the world, and also by a glimmer of hope that the Boston Marathon could help him get out of the pit he was in, Jacob turned himself over to the effort. Mike had told him he could lose one hundred pounds in just three months of training for a marathon, so Jacob bought a stationary bike and started pedaling. I should say here, if only for legal reasons, that attempting to lose one hundred pounds in three months is a terrible idea. Most experts say that a healthy rate of weight loss should be no more than one or two pounds a week.

"I knew it was a bad idea," Jacob told me on the phone, laughing. "I've made a life of bad ideas."

He hauled himself on top of a stationary bike for thirty minutes a day, then worked his way up to eight hours a day, sitting on that bike. Then running. The longest Jacob ran prior to the marathon was ten miles, which took him about three hours. And the weight dropped off. By the time he got to Hopkinton on Monday, April 16, 2007, he was down to 360 pounds, an astounding loss, just ten pounds short of his goal. (But, Jacob points out now, he lost ten pounds during the race, so he made it!) The crowd of qualified and then charity runners (myself somewhere in it) had long vanished down East Main Street out of Hopkinton, and Jacob and his three friends, Mike, Luke Webster, and Andrew Fleming, started out after them, into the cold, driving rain. (A fourth pal never appeared, until he showed up drunk in Kendall Square many, many miles later.)

"For the first few miles, I'd be running, and I'd see the water station ahead," Jacob remembers. "And then from a half mile away I could see them tearing it down."

266

There were no crowds, no Wellesley Scream Tunnel, no support. Instead, when he needed hydration or nutrition, Mike or Luke or Andrew would jump into a 7-Eleven and grab some bottles and bars. As I talked to Jacob, I began to realize that whether or not my marathon that day was more legitimate, his was a hell of a lot harder.

He got to the ten-mile marker — thankfully painted onto the asphalt, because all the signs had been removed — "on pace," at about three hours, but his race "fell apart" around mile 17. (In this, it turns out, Jacob and I did have something in common.) In his case, although his strength and breath were holding up, his feet were wrecked.

"I could barely walk," Jacob told me. "My feet weren't trained to endure the bone-crushing weight for that many hours. The last eight miles, I could either sprint or sit down. Sprinting seemed to take the weight off my feet. So I would sit a little, then I'd sprint, then I would have to sit down again. It took twice as long to do the last ten miles as it had the first ten. And we got lost in Brookline, and we ran an extra half mile or so."

But nonetheless, Jacob persisted. He and his friends slowly made their way down the sidewalks of Brookline and Boston, and then, just like every other Boston Marathoner, he sprinted down Boylston to the finish line — albeit hours after the race was over, and in the dark. Some guy in a bar yelled at him: "You think you're running the marathon?" And Jacob responded, "FUCK YEAH!"

And then he celebrated by hurrying back to law school in New Hampshire, where he had to perform the next morning in a mock court exam . . . on his feet, in quickly purchased shoes two sizes larger than his normal size, because his feet were so swollen.

Eight hours in the cold, wet, and dark — the weather had been so miserable that the organizers actually considered canceling the race — to end up with nothing to show for it but swollen feet. Did Jacob regret his run?

Absolutely not. "It was one of the best senses of accomplishment I've ever had."

Since that day in 2007, Jacob has managed, fitfully, to keep the weight off — he's at 350 pounds now — and has also kept running, but never again in a marathon. "Maybe I'll work my way down, the opposite way most people do it," he mused, laughing. "Start with a marathon, then a half, then a 10K, then a 5K, then I'll quit."

But he has had plenty to endure nonetheless. First Lyme disease, and then, practically the same day he got engaged, he got a call from his doctor saying, that headache that was bothering him? In fact, it was glioblastoma, the most virulent kind of brain tumor, the kind that killed Ted Kennedy a year later. Surprise! In the last few years, Jacob has been in and out of surgery, radiation, and chemo, gotten married, gotten his degree, gone to work — and then the cancer has recurred.

So Jacob has carried with him more burdens, handicaps, and bad luck than I — even poor pitiful I — could imagine. And, Jacob is certain, his remarkable, improbable run helps him get through his trials. "I can always look back on the most physically miserable day of my life and put things in perspective. If I'm feeling like shit, I can say I won't feel as shitty as I did at the end of that race." He's known around the chemotherapy infusion center as one of the more upbeat patients, he says, and after talking to him for an hour, I completely believe him.

Three months before the 2007 Boston Marathon, Jacob Seilheimer had a hard time climbing stairs. And yet he made it, enduring more than twice my time out in the wind and rain, suffering physical pain that would have stopped me cold, and doing it all for no medal, in front of no crowds — hell, he couldn't even really brag about it. But he said he would do it, so he did it. As he put it during his finish, "Fuck yeah!"

And so, standing by the side of the same road both of us had traversed at very different paces seven years earlier, I downed my third cup of Gatorade and decided I was feeling much better. Maybe I had been wrong. Maybe this wasn't the Cymbalta or withdrawal from it, maybe this was plain old dehydration — that causes dizziness, too. Dizziness that was now fading. My legs felt pretty good, fine even, especially considering I had just run fifteen miles. About four minutes had passed since I'd stopped running. I put down the fourth empty cup, thanked the volunteer, and took off. Could I catch them? Fuck yeah.

Erich was delighted at my return, certainly more for my sake than his. "I don't know what happened," I said, "but I'm fine now. Just needed some Gatorade, I guess." Monte was relieved I had arrived; he wanted to go a bit faster than Erich could at that point, and my return to my assigned job allowed him to run the race he wanted. We said goodbye, and I again took hold of my end of the tether, and led Erich Manser toward the first of the Newton Hills.

But now, as I had a new birth of energy, Erich was fading. The heat was beating down on his head, bare amid the circular strap of his visor, and while his grin remained, it was becoming something more like a grimace with every step. I knew — even on short acquaintance — that he would never quit, so instead of suggesting dropping out or even a rest stop, I started doing the one thing I could do: I started talking. I told him about my running career, and how I started late in life and did things I couldn't have imagined earlier on; I told him about *Wait Wait . . . Don't Tell Me!,* about Paula Poundstone (yes, that's what she's like; no, I just pretend to get upset with her, I really love her), about Carl Kasell. I told him the story of one of my earliest meetings with Carl, back in the first few months when we did the show from remote studios and I hardly saw him. Carl and I were posing for publicity photos in an NPR performance studio, and as we stood there in our sport jackets I looked around for something more interesting to do. There was a grand piano in the corner. We pulled it out and Carl clambered on top of it while I sat down at the keyboard, a la Michelle Feiffer and Jeff

Bridges in *The Fabulous Baker Boys*. Carl put his chin in his hands and blinked at me while I pretended to play. "I've always wanted to do this," Carl said.

"Sweet," said Erich.

"Got another hill coming up," I said.

"Sweet," said Erich.

We shuffled up the second and third hills, and finally the fourth, Heartbreak Hill, slowing down the whole time. By the time we reached Boston College, Erich was reacting to almost anything I said with the single word "sweet." I thought about testing him. How does vinegar taste, Erich?

Then he said something else. "Every time we go under something, it goes pitch black," he said. "Could you please warn me?"

Gone under something? What? I looked back — we had passed under a photography bridge, a temporary platform built over the course for official photographers to take souvenir race photos of participants. I had hardly noticed it. I don't think I even looked up to smile. But even passing through that narrow, faint shadow — seven or eight feet wide at the most — had momentarily turned off the lights for Erich. "Gotcha, man," I said. "Sorry I missed that one."

"Sweet," he said.

We were into the last five miles, through

the streets of Brookline and Boston. With the increased urban density, there were more overpasses, more tall buildings next to the course, more shadows. I concentrated on calling out each one to Erich, while still firmly holding on to my end of the tether. I had returned to the feeling of focus I had the prior year with William; I couldn't be bothered to think about how tired or hot I might have been; I was too busy doing my job. I was once again the watcher on the walls of men, the last best hope of Earth, the catcher in the rye.

We passed my uncle and aunt at the same spot we had seen them last year, but my parents were nowhere in sight. (It turns out that they were caught behind the new security fencing, and watched me from the other side of the road.) Erich managed a wave but continued to concentrate mostly on putting one foot in front of the other. He was slowing even more. At a number of points, I stopped running myself, slowing to a quick walk so as not to get too far ahead of him.

"Three miles to go, Erich."

"Sweet."

We passed the mile-24 marker. At this point last year, William had been falling apart, stopping to walk every three hundred yards or so. Erich showed no sign of doing that, just a steady, gradual slowing as the heat beat down . . . except now he was speeding up again. He looked ahead, peering into the distance with his failing eyes. He said the first words other than "sweet" for at least four miles.

"My family," he said.

There they were, his wife, Lisa, and their two young daughters, Ellie and Grace Margaret, on the other side of the temporary metal fencing. The girls shrieked with delight: "Daddy! Daddy!" Erich ran up to them and said "I need kisses!" and embraced them, getting his kisses, one by one, and then all at once. He quickly introduced me: his oldest daughter has the same name as my middle daughter. I looked at how Erich, nearly blind, looked at his daughters. He handed me his phone and asked me to take his picture. I looked on the screen at how his daughters looked at him. I took the picture. I handed him back his phone.

I stood apart and waited. I could have waited all day, and watched.

Erich told me later that he wanted to stay there, too. "I remember sinking into that embrace, and not wanting to leave it," he said. "I had to force myself."

I led him away with the tether. He turned

and waved once and moved on.

"You're a lucky man," I said.

"Don't I know it," he said.

"Sweet," I said.

There was nothing left in Erich's tank, or mine, so the right turn onto Hereford, the left onto Boylston, was done at the same slogging pace we had kept up since leaving Erich's family. Boylston Street, the site of the bombing, was packed with spectators, even this late into the day, all of whom had defied recent history and endured rings of security and metal detectors to show that Boston was not only Strong but Stubborn. And loud. They shouted and cheered. The finish line appeared ahead, and as it always does, seemed to take its damn sweet time getting to us. We crossed the line and embraced.

We walked forward and in a moment were at the spot of pavement where I had been standing when the bombs went off. I turned around and looked back, again, at the finish line superstructure, the backs of TV cameras, the cops — so many cops — the people crowding the course on both sides vanishing into the distance back to the second bombing site and beyond. Nothing happened. Other than the cheers, and the PA announcer and the runners shouting with joy and relief as they finished the Boston Marathon, defying their own limitations and the two sons of bitches who had tried to kill it, other than that happy cacophony, there was silence.

"C'mon," said Erich. "I want to go meet my family."

So did I.

"Of course," I said. And then, like war heroes, like Olympic champions, like Luke and Han (but not Chewie), we received medals draped over our necks. "That was tough," Erich said.

"Yeah but . . . we made it."

POSTSCRIPT

These days, I don't run as far or as fast as I used to, but I still run every day. The dogs demand it.

I could never have a dog while married; my ex-wife was deathly allergic to them. Now there are two. Dee Dee is a whippet mix and therefore was born, or at least bred, to run. She flattens her ears to her aerodynamic skull and zips along so smoothly I could rest a coffee cup on her back. Dutchie, though, is a German shepherd and pit bull mix, and seemingly had no natural inclination to run when we first adopted her. But after watching and imitating Dee Dee on a few short expeditions, she's become a lunatic for it. She tugs at the leash as her legs flail, panting and pulling, her tongue so far out she could taste the sidewalk if she lowered her head a tad. She's not skinny, not fast, just stubborn and absolutely determined to run as fast as she can until she collapses. She reminds me of myself, once upon a time.

They've learned to wait while I have my coffee and get my juices — and other things — flowing, but after thirty minutes they get antsy and excited and start jumping up in my lap as I sit at the kitchen table in my new house, and they run to the door and back, and when I finally get up and pick up their collars, they go from excited to berserk, leaping up to throw their heads through the collars in midair and thereby saving a second of preparation. Collars on, they run to the front foyer, paw at the running belt and leashes, and whine at the door until it's open. Outside, finally, they pull me down the street like Ben-Hur's chariot horses. Sometimes, I will confess, it's a pain in the ass, as well as the lower back, and I'm sure one of these days I'm going to trip just as they see a squirrel across a busy street and I will depart this earth, leaving behind the kind of hilarious obituary I've always wanted.

Sometimes, Dee Dee, Dutchie, and I run the half mile or so to that old Victorian house that I had planned on being the last home I ever owned. My kids still spend most of their time there, along with their mother and stepfather. I haven't been in it, or even stood on the porch, in about two years, since the time we finalized our divorce, which itself was three years after my moving out. I don't miss it; while there are many happy memories there, they are buried in the past under more recent, less pleasant ones. The dogs and I keep going.

We rarely, if ever, make it all the way to the town house I sold soon after the divorce was final. It never felt, even with the walls covered with kid photos and memorabilia of my disrupted life, like a home. It felt like a way station, a waiting room between my former life and my next, and I was tired of waiting. Now I live in a smallish bungalow, built in 1923 and renovated a hundred times since then, sometimes (judging from the screws popping out of the moldings, for example) quite poorly. I didn't like the town house because it was so new, so sterile; it had no character. Now I live in a home with character literally falling off the ceiling, requiring a minimum expenditure of $500 to glue it back on. But: it's close to where my daughters live, it's got a yard for the dogs, and Mara really likes it.

Dee Dee had come into my life with Mara, a package deal. Like me, Mara had come to a moment in her life when human relationships seemed impenetrably difficult and profoundly unsatisfying, so she visited an animal shelter near where she was living in Oregon, where, she says, she saw a little trembling creature in the back who seemed to have the same opinion about people as she did. She introduced herself, they got along, and now Mara and Dee Dee are as inseparable a pair as Lyra and her daemon in Philip Pullman's novels. I realize, and accept, that whatever happens between myself and Mara, I will always be, at best, a close second to Dee Dee in her affections. She demurs, saying we're tied for first, and I'm ready to believe it, but I will be careful to avoid situations in which she would have to choose between us. If we all end up on a cruise together, for example, I'm going to make sure the lifeboats, or floating doors, are capacious.

Back in late 2014, almost two years after my marriage ended in fact if not in law, I was still accepting almost any invitation that came my way, even though there was no one else living in my town house whom I needed to avoid. One came from The Second City, inviting me to be a special guest — *Andy Williams Christmas Show*–style — in a parody of *A Christmas Carol* called *Twist Your Dickens*. I was given the name of the stage manager and told to arrange with her my arrival on the night of the performance. That stage manager, a strikingly beautiful woman with an exceptionally professional mien, was a tad wary of me, as it turned out, from dealing with various amateur special guest stars with inflated senses of their own importance. The special guest the prior night had wandered around the sacrosanct backstage area, talking loudly, playing with the props, and putting on wigs. So the stage manager carefully and clearly told me what to do and where to stand before I did it, a good five feet from anything I could break.

I waited quietly, with my hands safely in my pockets, for the show to begin. "Five minutes, Mr. Sagal," said the stage manager.

"Thank you, five," I responded, as theater tradition dictated. She raised an eyebrow, and nodded in approval.

It may well be that I owe my present and future happiness to the fact that the "celebrity" who had preceded me the night before was a complete asshole.

The stage manager and I talked for an hour after the show that night, as the cast finished their drinks and deserted us one by one, and again two nights later when I came back to visit her in her booth from which she looked down on the production like

Hera on Olympus, ready to cast thunder-bolts if her gentle instructions were ignored. Then another evening still, and we found ourselves once again in a bar with the cast and this time they all left with a little more purpose, as if clearing the stage, smiling back at her as they went.

It was time for The Conversation, one I felt obligated to start. I explained to the stage manager that I was going through the Divorce From Hell, that three teenage girls were involved, that I was in no position to offer anyone anything like a serious or lasting relationship, but that I liked her and thought it would be fun to spend time together. I didn't expect her to throw her drink in my face — stage managers prefer to leave theatrics to actors — but I did expect her to look at her watch and bring down the curtain.

Instead, she told me that she felt exactly the same way. She had recently gotten out of a bad relationship that left her with even less appetite for such things and was in fact relieved that I wouldn't ask her to be serious or committed or even around much, if she didn't feel like it. It felt like a fortunate meeting of like-minded individuals. We might have shaken hands on it.

The next night, her night off, I invited her

over for dinner.

"Can I bring my dog?" asked Mara.

"Of course," I said.

She's told me more than once in the years since then that if I had said no, that would have been the end of it. One of the odd things about homes: you don't realize you have one until one day you're in it. Sometimes it comes with a dog. Sometimes it invites you to bring your dog.

Once Mara and Dee Dee moved in to the little house — or is it Dee Dee and Mara? — we realized we couldn't deny Dee Dee the pleasure we enjoyed from having a dog to play with, so we started looking around for a second dog. Dutchie — named by her rescuers, who thought, incorrectly, she was a Dutch shepherd — was found in the January cold on the west side of Chicago, her teats filled with milk, desperately mewling and scratching at a door of an apartment building, where no one admitted to knowing anything about her. The shelter volunteers who spent two days trying to catch her assumed that she had been bred for a litter and then tossed into the street to die; certainly, whatever had happened to her had completely soured her on the concept of human kindness. Unable to get close enough to the skittish dog to catch her, the volunteers put an old couch in the alley near where she hid so she'd at least have a place to rest. They checked the next day, and somebody had stolen the couch. Maybe Dutchie was right about humans.

Eventually, they lured her in with food and brought her to the vet for medical treatment. She healed up, learned slowly to trust again, and started revealing a surprising enthusiasm for everyone she met — humans, dogs, cats, basically everything but squirrels. Her inner doggish faith in goodness overwhelms the evidence of her own experience, and sometimes I envy her.

So one last refugee from a broken family joined our home, completing — for now — our new one.

Mara is not a runner, although sometimes she enjoys riding her bike alongside us as the dogs drag me down the street like an Inuit sled. She grew up a figure skater and a dancer, so her view on exercise is that it has to have some aesthetic point to it. But she tolerates my insatiable need to run around outside for an hour or so every day because she knows the person who returns from these sojourns, as sweaty and smelly as he may be, is happier than the person who left.

Mara, unlike my ex-wife, is Jewish, so we recently celebrated our first Hanukkah in the new/old house, and so for the first time in many years we sang the prayers — odd how we can still remember them from Hebrew school decades before — and I helped light the menorah, and we let it light up the window, a small riposte to the thousands of Christmas lights and the inflatable Santa in the yard next door. During our first Christmas season in the house I would sometimes go for a run in the afternoon and come back in the darkness, looking for the small menorah candles amid the greater glow of our *goyische* neighbors, a quiet sign that, as the letters on the dreidel indicate, *Nes Gadol Hayah Sham,* a great miracle happened here.

I ran as a guide in 2015 at Boston for Erich Manser again, this time along with another guide, because I was afraid I wouldn't be able to make it the whole distance. I was (kind of) right: I had to stop for an egress at about mile 24, and didn't quite catch up with the two of them before they crossed the line a minute ahead of me. That was my last marathon for a while, as I found myself slipping a bit, both in terms of fitness and dedication to the sport. But with the help of Mara and the dogs, I remain on the road, and here I intend to stay, no matter how slowly I might travel down it.

The problem with being a midlife crisis runner is you start your transformation just as everything else in your body is going to hell. Inside this fifty-three-year-old body is a thirteen-year-old runner, and as much as he would like to, he can't get out. That poor kid is like the John Cusack character at the end of *Being John Malkovich,* peering out of eyes he can't control. It seems unfair, actually. That ambitious youngster looking out through my tired eyes deserves better than me. I feel kind of bad for him.

The man who trained for and ran a 3:09 marathon in 2011 is gone; there are some days when I glance at a shop window as I run by and see someone who looks like that guy, but if I stop to make sure, he vanishes, because I am standing still, and he never was. The loss has not been so much ability but focus and desire; now, far more than otherwise, when the urge to stop comes upon me, I give in.

So I am a middle-aged man, born in 1965, and I am a runner, born (after some false starts) in 2005, and that is what I shall be until both pass on, some indeterminate time from now, at the same moment. I've come too far to retrace my steps now. The kind of runner I will be, in the next decade, and the one after that, will be different: less competitive with himself or others, less eager to find new worlds to conquer, but also less obsessed and less narrowly focused on the next square of pavement ahead. Runners slow, and runners fail. Some are grinded away by the friction on knees or feet, or a chronic lung or heart problem; some unlucky bastards are knocked down on the road. But the mark of a runner is to always get up.

My relationship with my own three daughters was profoundly changed through the trauma of the divorce, and remains so. But like Erich Manser, I have a kind of tunnel vision, looking forward to the day when we can all look at one another with new eyes. It's not a sprint, but a marathon, and I'm good at those.

People ask me about the benefits of running, and there are many, even more than the ones discussed in this book, and I have realized many of them — better health, increased energy, the deep-seated thrill of setting a goal and, through difficult work, surpassing it. I have run many miles in many different places with many different people, and each one was worth the effort. But if there's one thing that I have gained from my running career, it's not the strength or cardiovascular fitness to run ten or twenty-six miles at a time, but the patience and focus to stay in the mile I'm in. Run long enough, and everything comes into view, be it a finish line or a home, a new one or one remade. What running has given me, most of all, is the practice of persistence.

And maybe, too, a habit of hope. Running sometimes sucks, but every run ends, and tomorrow is a new opportunity to take a first step. The differences between running as a lifestyle and "jogging" as exercise are many and much debated, but the key one is this: You "jog" as necessary exercise, something to endure. You run with the expectation that this outing, today, will be the day when it all comes together, when instead of your feet propelling you along the ground you're actually flying, and your feet only serve to keep you anchored to the ground. Joggers wait to finish; we runners expect to get somewhere.

Which might be why, after some hesitation, I recently put aside the traumas of the past and the fear that I might repeat them in the future, and asked Mara to marry me. She said yes, and in that moment I once again experienced the same joy I did on the occasion of the birth of each of my three daughters. It felt as if a new life was beginning, and all kinds of wonderful things might happen. There is a celebration in committing yourself to a particular future.

The old joke is that a second marriage is the triumph of hope over experience. I disagree (of course I do): a second marriage is, or should be, like good luck, the residue of preparation. I had twenty years of training in how not to engage in human relationships. Like my first marathon, I did everything wrong. But now, with better training, with practice, with a learned realism about the road ahead of me, I'm confident about achieving a good time. I will be reckless and say I expect to medal.

Relationships may have something in common with running, in that you can practice and study and think and train and suffer and regroup, and learn from your mistakes and improve, and learn to avoid what pains you can and live with the ones you can't, but in the end, all of that doesn't matter. The only thing that really matters is whom you choose to do it with, and whom you do it for. As I said, we are cruelest to ourselves. When somebody else is counting on us, somebody we don't want to disappoint, well then we get up early. We show up. We put our own struggle out of our mind and focus on the other person, and all of a sudden our feet no longer touch the ground.

There is sadness, and there is hate, and bitterness. There is regret and fear and doubt and there are the injuries done to us and there are the injuries we do to others. But the lesson and practice of running is, again, a faith in the possibility of positive change. That, if you run enough miles, with enough dedication and the right kind of mind-set, if you accept the limitations of what's possible but refuse to accept the rutted path of what's painless, if you keep at it, if you keep going, you can become what it was you were meant to be.

I've run around the earth, maybe more than once, and I'm still right where I started. But everything else has changed, and so much doubt and pain and struggle has fallen away, so that the only thing left to me, of all the things that weighed me down when I began that circumnavigation, is love. Love isn't fast, and it isn't strong. It's stubborn, though, and it has muscles you can see. It can't overwhelm doubt and it can't banish bitterness and it can't prevent anger and it can't hold back despair, which have so many times risen up to overwhelm me,

my life, and my family.
But love can outlast them all.

ACKNOWLEDGMENTS

This book could not have been written without:

At *Runner's World:* David Willey, who invited me to write for the magazine, as well as my editors, John Atwood, Charlie Butler, and Sean Downey, as well as Lindsay Bender, Mark Remy, Jennifer Van Allen, Amby Burfoot, and Pam Nisevich.

At the Boston Marathon: Josh Warren and his colleagues at Team With A Vision and the Massachusetts Association for the Blind and Visually Impaired, and fellow marathoners William Greer, Erich Manser, Joe De-Gutis, Ron Abramson, Dan Streetman, Aaron Scheidies, Corvin Bazgan, and Monte Harvill. Thanks also to Ellen Greer.

My running group, who saw me through many miles and much else: Chris Sheean,

Chris Weber, Chris Courtois, Arden Swanson, Paul Olszowka, Paula O'Connor, Perry Vietti, Doug Schenkelberg, Doug Schaller, Martin Nieman, John Friesen, Candelario Celio, Ken Kansa, Alona Banai, and Ron Burke. My thanks as well to the Oak Park Running Club.

At NPR: Doug Berman, Michael Danforth, Eric Nuzum, Ian Chillag, Miles Doornboss, Emily Ecton, Jennifer Mills, Bill Kurtis and Donna LaPietra, Adam Felber, Paula Poundstone, P. J. O'Rourke, Alonzo Bodden, Peter Grosz, Faith Salie, Roxanne Roberts, Tom Bodett, Mo Rocca, Luke Burbank, Brian Babylon, and all our other panelists and staff members.

My editor, Jofie Ferrari-Adler, who showed extraordinary kindness and patience long after I should have exhausted it. My gratitude to him and the team at Simon & Schuster, including Jonathan Karp, Richard Rhorer, Stephen Bedford, Julia Prosser, Julianna Haubner, Kristen Lemire, Jonathan Evans, Carla Benton, Sara Kitchen, Kayley Hoffman, Beth Maglione, Ruth Lee-Mui, Alison Forner, and David Litman.

My literary agent, Luke Janklow, and his executive officer, Claire Dippel.

The remarkable Misty DeMars and her family.

My early readers: Paul Schellinger, Amy Dickinson, Roy Blount Jr., Alex Kotlowitz, and Erin Hogan.

Randy Wayne White and his friend Doc Ford, who generously lent me their home as a writer's retreat.

Michael Hawley of the EG Conference and Jenifer Hixson of the Moth, who helped me present spoken-word versions of chapter one. I would not have survived from one bombing to the next without very many friends who provided kindnesses large and small, including Ellen and Paul Coffey, Bob Haft and Deb Fausti, Deann and Rick Bayless, Paul Schellinger and Mindy Thomas, Tim Bent, Pete and Amanda Docter, Stephen and Denise Weeks, Lisa Mount, Michael Johnson and Max Temkin. There were many others and to list all of them would double the length of this book. Suffice to say: if you shared a kind word with me, I remember it and I am grateful to you all.

Kyle Cassidy, my padawan, for many different author photos, including the one on the cover of the original publisher's edition.

Cris Hammond, Dave Pettus, Kenneth Goldman, and all the gentlemen of the forest.

My closest friends for more than thirty years: Jess Bravin and Nicole Galland.

My family, who I hope will not mind their appearances here, most especially my father, whose story I presume to tell.

My daughters, Rose, Grace, and Willa: there was a time I ran with all of you, pushing you or running alongside your bikes. I keep running so I may find you on the road again.

And finally: Mara, my wife, my happy ending, my destination, my home. Turns out I was running toward you the whole time.

ABOUT THE AUTHOR

Peter Sagal is the host of the Peabody Award–winning NPR news quiz *Wait Wait . . . Don't Tell Me!,* the most popular show on public radio, heard by more than five million listeners each week. He is also a playwright, a screenwriter, the host of *Constitution USA with Peter Sagal* on PBS, a onetime extra in a Michael Jackson music video, a contributor to publications from *Opera News* to *AARP The Magazine,* and he has spent ten years as a featured columnist in *Runner's World.* He's run fourteen marathons across the United States. Sagal lives near Chicago with his wife, Mara.

The employees of Thorndike Press hope you have enjoyed this Large Print book. All our Thorndike, Wheeler, and Kennebec Large Print titles are designed for easy reading, and all our books are made to last. Other Thorndike Press Large Print books are available at your library, through selected bookstores, or directly from us.

For information about titles, please call:
  (800) 223-1244

or visit our website at:
  gale.com/thorndike

To share your comments, please write:
Publisher
Thorndike Press
10 Water St., Suite 310
Waterville, ME 04901